BOTTLE CAP ACTIVITIES
Recreational Recycling

Kathy Cisneros

DELIVERING THE BEST RESOURCES TO EDUCATORS
HUMANICS ™
LEARNING

HUMANICS LEARNING
P.O. Box 7400
Atlanta, Georgia 30357

BOTTLE CAP

ACTIVITIES

Recreational Recycling

HUMANICS™ **LEARNING**

HUMANICS LEARNING
PO Box 7400
Atlanta, Georgia 30357-0400

First Printing 1998

PRINTED IN THE UNITED STATES OF AMERICA

ISBN 0-89334-279-3

Library of Congress Cataloging-in-Publication Data

Cisneros, Kathy
Bottle cap activities: recreational recycling/ by Kathy Cisneros.
     p. cm.
     ISBN 0-89334-279-3 (pbk.) -- ISBN 0-89334-282-3 (library)
     1. Plastic bottle craft. 2. Creative activities and seatwork.
I. Title.
TT297.C57 1998
745.5--dc21
                                      98-12414
                                        CIP

DEDICATION

This book is dedicated to my children Ricky and Valerie
who are my future,
to my mom who never gave up on me,
to my dad who encouraged me to pursue my dreams,
to my sisters Betty and Toni who took the time to listen,
to my friends Debbie, Margaret, Patsy and Emily
who never let me give up on myself,
to my Aunt Bettina who inspired me with her love of animals and the earth,
to my kindred cousin Kris who shares my love for writing and creativity,
to my music partner Lynn Darden
who brought life to the play with her music and dedication to children,
and to Mike Angel who has my *colors* and my songs
and for everyone else who believes:

Tomorrow's Children
will live and play
Within the world we mold today
What we do and how we live
Will determine what we give.
By changing how we think and learn,
We'll have so much more to give in return.
We'll give them a chance,
to live as we do.
It's all in your hands,
It's all up to YOU!

TABLE OF CONTENTS:

Chapter 3
The Bottle Cap Barnyard Crafts

Chapter 4
Games

Chapter 5
Musical Play

Chapter 6
The Bottle Cap Musical Play

BOTTLE CAP ACTIVITIES

Welcome to Recreational Recycling

Parents and teachers can accumulate plastic bottle caps and other household items to create useful crafts that can be educational as well as decorative.By collecting, cleaning and sorting the various items, You'll have an abundance of recycling resources available for FREE!

In creating this book along with the musical program, it was my goal to educate people on the various ways we can utilize non-recyclable plastic bottle caps rather than filling the landfills with them. By making use of this durable plastic for toys, games and decorations, we can turn a problem into a *solution*.

Plastic bottle caps accumulate quickly and can be a valuable resource for teachers, camp counslers, daycare centers, boy and girl scout organizations and senior citizen homes who may have limited funding but require a large number crafts.

In additon, plastic bottle caps can be used for fund raising events and church bazaars. Following simple, easy to read, step by step instructions and large detailed graphics, these crafts are fun for environmentalists from 8 to 80!

School teachers will find the musical the BOTTLE CAP KIDS an innovative and educational Earth Day Play. By accumulating the caps at the beginning of the school year, children can design the costumes and posters and projects in Art class in time for the traditional Earth Day in April. The script is easy and fun to learn since the entire play is in rhyme! This is a unique way to encourage children to be creative as well as environmentally aware.

The bottle cap yo-yo is the perfect project for your fifth grader. This student will learn how to combine engineering, art, science and recycling all in one project!

You have the materials readily available and the instructions to turn these toss aways into treasures! Follow these collection procedures and have fun Bottle Cap Crafting!

To my children, Ricky and Valerie
for whom I live:
You can change what you see!
Recycle like me!
The bottle caps show you the way.
Just empower the kids!
Pop the tops!
Save the lids!
For tomorrow begins here today.

Love
Kathy Cisneros

NOTES

CHAPTER 1

The
Bottle
Cap

Planning

&

Preparing

NOTES

PLEASE ACCUMULATE THE FOLLOWING FOR BOTTLE CAP CRAFTING

1. Plastic bottle caps (any size, shape, color)

2. Plastic break away rings around the caps

3. White or blue liners gently pried from inside of the plastic bottle caps

4. Dishwashing liquid caps

5. Fabric softner cups

6. Bell shaped shampoo and mouthwash caps

7. 2-liter bottles cut in half at the middle seam

8. Laundry scoop detergent cups

9. Popsicle sticks

10. Plastic grocery bags (all colors)

CLEANING PROCEDURES

1. Wash and dry all plastic bottles and bottle caps in warm soapy water.

2. Let items air dry on a paper towel overnight before crafting.

Seperate your craft collection into containers for easy access

Plastic rings	Bottle Caps	Plastic Bottles	Laundry Scoops	Liners

HOT AIR EGGSHELL BALLOON EGG PREPARATION PROCEDURES

ADULT SUPERVISION NEEDED

1. Use a safety pin to twist a small hole at the top of the eggshell.

2. Cover the hole with your finger and make a larger hole at the bottom.

3. Gently blow the contents into a plastic bag for later cooking use or freezing.

4. Run water through the eggshell until the water runs clear.

5. Let dry on a paper towel overnight.

6. Accumulate your clean, empty eggshells and store for crafting.

SUPPLIES TO HAVE ON HAND FOR BOTTLE CAP CRAFTING

Tacky Glue

Glitter

Fabric paints

Ribbon roses

Yarn or cord

Pom poms

Low melt glue gun

Felt

Low melt glue sticks

Q-tips

Polka dot Fabric

Lace

Loopy chenille

Spools

Scissors

Twine

Stickers

Twist ties

Seasonal miniatures

Ribbon

Also break down cereal boxes and save the wax paper inside to protect your work environment.

CUTTING THE PLASTIC BOTTLE
ADULT SUPERVISON IS NEEDED

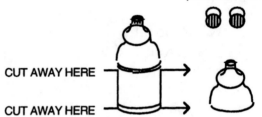

plastic bottle caps

CUT AWAY HERE →

CUT AWAY HERE →

WHEN A GLUE IS NEEDED TO MAKE THE CRAFTS
ADULT SUPERVISON IS NEEDED

pop off top portion

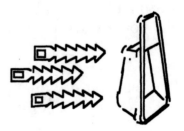

14

ALTERNATIVE PROCEDURE

1. For younger crafters who would like to make the dolls but are unable to cut the bottles, there are alternative procedures.

2. You can create any of the bodies to the bottle cap dolls by using folded cereal boxes.

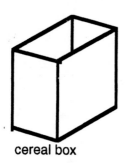

cereal box

3. Open the cereal box at the seams and lay it flat. Follow the instructions shown then replace the folded cereal box *body* for the bottle.

cereal box

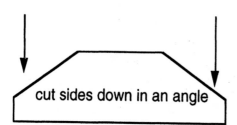

cut sides down in an angle

fold into a cone and glue at the seam

ALTERNATIVE TO CORDING

1. For those who may have difficulty cording the caps, there is a simplified procedure.

2. Use the low melt glue gun to glue strips of felt (any color) to the outside diameter of each cap in the project.

felt

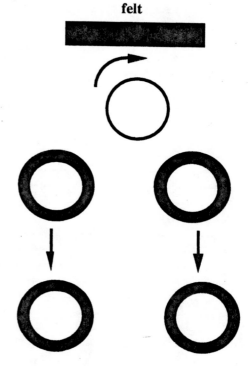

3. Use a low melt glue gun to glue each felted bottle cap together.

4. Complete the project as instructed.

NOTES

CHAPTER 2

The Bottle Cap

Calendar Of Crafts

NOTES

JANUARY

BOTTLE CAP CLOCK

TO MAKE THIS CRAFT YOU NEED

1 large transparent plastic coffee can lid
1 push pin
2 yellow plastic garbage bag twist ties
Black fabric paint

TO BEGIN

1. Push the push pin through the square opening of each twist tie.

2. Push the pin and the twist ties through the plastic lid and secure in place in the back.

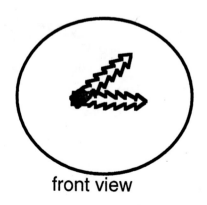

front view

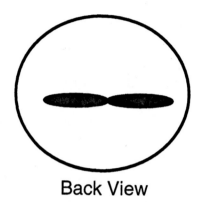

Back View

3. Use fabric paint to decorate the face of the clock with numbers. Rotate the hands freely around the face when the paint dries.

**TIME
TO
RECYCLE!**

BOTTLE CAP BABY CARRIAGE

TO MAKE THIS CRAFT YOU NEED

1 plastic Laundry Scoop
4 plastic bottle caps (same size same color)
6 inches of yarn or string
Black fabric paint
1 large sewing needle
1 large paper cup holder
1 chenille stem (any color)

TO BEGIN

1. Set the laundry scoop on a table with the flat side down.

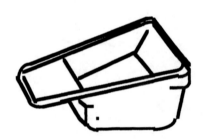

3. Tie a large knot at one end of the string. String the other end of the string through the large eye needle.

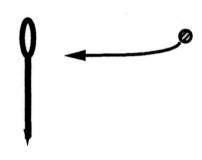

4. Push the needle through the midde of the first bottle cap and pull the knot until it reaches the flat surface of the cap.

5. Continue pushing the needle and thread through the front side end of the laundry scoop, through the middle and out the opposite side. Push the needle through the hollowside of the second cap. Tie a knot and secure. The wheels should rotate freely. Repeat this procedure with the back end of the scoop using the last two caps.

6. Fold the paper cupcake in half. Using a low melt glue gun, secure it in place across the wide end of the scoop.

6. Bend a chenille stem into a square handle and glue to opposite ends of the small square at the front of the scoop.

NOTES

FEBRUARY

JEWELRY COLLECTION
POP TOP PENDANTS

If you look within, each garbage bin,
to see what was left behind,
You wouldn't believe,
what people just leave,
The waste would just blow your mind!
The people should learn, reuse and return,
Rethink! Stop the excess from growing,
See how you can change it,
Start new! Rearrange it.
Recycle before you start throwing!
Take a 2-liter top, plastic from pop,
Some yarn, some glitter, and glue,
Enhance and embellish,
And soon you will relish,
A pendant created by you!

TO MAKE THESE CRAFTS YOU NEED:

3 Two-liter plastic bottle cap
1 top off a dishwashing liquid bottle
Glitter (any color of preference)
22" of Metallic bead cord or yarn
          (any color)
1 chenille stem (any color)
Tacky Glue
Glitter
Terrycloth ponytail holder
Low melt glue gun with adult
supervision

TO BEGIN

1. Select one 2-liter plastic bottle cap
    from your clean and dried craft
    collection.

2. Place a generous amount
    of Tacky glue in the
    empty hollow. Using a
    Q-tip, swirl it around
    the inside until all the
    exposed areas of the side
    and bottom are coverered.

3. Fill the cap with glitter up
    to the rim. Turn the cap
    over a folded piece of
    paper and tap the back of
    the bottle cap to catch
    the loose excess.
               LET DRY

4. Spread Tacky glue along
    the outside rim of
    the bottle cap until all
    exposed areas are
    covered. Wipe the excess
    glue away and dry your
    hands.

10. Glue a ribbon rose or bow at the top to cover the knot.

5. Press the end of metallic bead cord or yarn into the edge of the cap. Begin rotating the cord/ yarn around the cap until you've reached the middle of the two caps.   STOP!

BOTTLE CAP BRACELET OR HAIR BOW

6. Make a 20" loop with the cord/ yarn and tie a simple slip knot at the base of the loop.

7. Pull tightly on the cord to shrink and center the knot.

8. Continue rotating the cord/ yarn around the cap until you've reached the edge. Snip the cord and secure in place at the edge with glue.

9. Glue gathered lace around the corded cap to embellish.
(optional)

1. Follow the steps for making a pop-top pendant but skip the loop! Glue your finished cap to the top of a terry cloth pony tail holder. Wrap the finished product around your wrist or your pony tail!

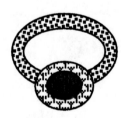

DISHWASHER DINNER RING

TO BEGIN

1. Select a plastic push-pull top from a bottle of dishwashing liquid.

2. Separate the top half from the bottom. Save the bottom half for dishwasher dolls, pencil puppets and pop-top people.

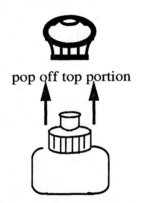

pop off top portion

3. For this craft you need only the top peak portion.

4. Select any color chenille stem and cut it in half. Fold it in half again and set it aside.

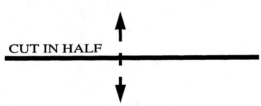

CUT IN HALF

5. Turn the top peak over so that the wide part is facing you.

6. Under parental supervision, use the low melt glue gun to fill up the open chamber with warm glue.

Fill opening with glue

7. Quickly insert the the chenille stem into the opening until it will go no further

Quickly insert stem

8. Bend the chenille stem into an adjustable ring that will fit any finger!

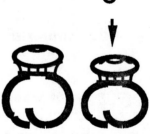

9. Paint the top of your ring with Fabric Paint or plain Tacky Glue. Sprinkle with glitter for sparkle. LET DRY.

10. Glue a ribbon rose, birthstone, tiny pom-pom or gem-stone to the top to embellish!

BOTTLE CAP BEADS

TO MAKE THIS CRAFT YOU NEED

20 push-pull dishwashing liquid tops
16 to 18 inches of yarn or string
Tacky glue
Glitter

TO BEGIN

1. Pull the tops off each dishwashing
    liquid cap.

pop off top portion

2. Wash and dry each top.

3. Cut the yarn or string to the
    desired length.

4. String the beads in a row to
    create a necklace from
    the bottle cap beads.

5. Vary the designs by placing
    some tops from back to bac

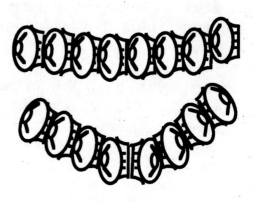

6. String the beads over and
    through a chenille stem to
    create a bracelet.

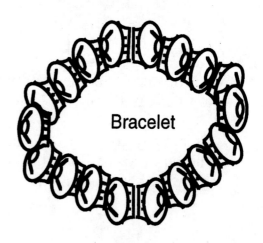

Bracelet

7. You can string a single bead
    face up on string or yarn
    and glue a fashion bead to
    the center hole. Paint and
    glitter your pendant to
    embellish.

BOTTLE CAP BOW TIE BOX

Don't forget Dad, on Valentine's Day,
Show him you love him,
the recycling way.
Create a BowTie Box that he can keep.
Fill it with candies and goodies so deep.
Use bottle caps, a shoe box and felt,
This kind of treasure,
is one that won't melt!

TO MAKE THIS CRAFT YOU NEED

1 empty shoe box
Black Felt
White Felt
Tacky Glue
Black Fabric Paint
3 Plastic bottle caps
1 bag of Dad's favorite candy
1 small white 2 liter top

TO BEGIN

1. Cover the outside of the entire box with black felt. Use tacky glue to secure the felt in place.   (LET DRY)

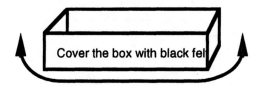
Cover the box with black felt

2. Cover the lid with black felt and secure in place with Tacky glue.

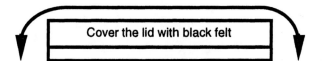
Cover the lid with black felt

3. Cut a triangle of white felt the same width and the same length as the shoe box lid

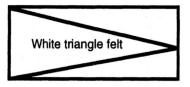
White triangle felt

4. Cut a bow tie from black felt and glue it to the white triangle. Glue a small white white 2 liter top to the center of the tie.

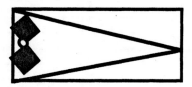

5. Glue three plastic bottle caps down the front of the triangle for buttons. Use black fabric paint to color them black. **Let Dry.**

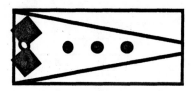

6. Fill the bottle cap bow tie box with dad's favorite candy! Add a special letter to the box that tells dad how much he means to you!

27

NOTES

MARCH

LADY LEPRECHAUN

This lady leprechaun
has magical charms,
A bottle cap rainbow
held tight in her arms.
Long flowing hair,
flaming bright red,
Glued to the top
of her bottle cap head!!
Three leaf clovers
and a pot full of gold,
You'll love this
leprechaun,
To keep and to hold!!

TO MAKE THIS CRAFT YOU NEED

1   two liter plastic skirt shaped bottle
2   large (milk or O.J.) plastic bottle
      caps
12 x5 piece of green lacy material
6 different colored plastic bottle caps
Black fabric paint
Green fabric paint
Tacky Glue
Low melt glue gun
      adult supervision
1 square of light green felt
small clover embellishments
Red loopy chenille or red yarn for hair

TO BEGIN

1. Cut the plastic bottle in half at the
     skirt shaped seam.

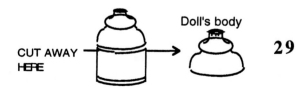

CUT AWAY
HERE

Doll's body

29

2. Glue the plastic caps together
    with tacky glue and set aside to
    dry.

plastic bottle caps   Glue Bottle caps together

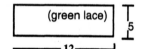

3. Begin at the back of the bottle
    half and glue the green lace in
    repeating pleats at the neck rim
    until your reach the opposite
    side.

(green lace) ⊺ 5

—12—
Begin at the back and pleat as you go for a full dress

4. Once you've secured the lace
    along the back with the glue
    gun, glue the dried bottle caps
    on top of the lace at the rim
    for the head.

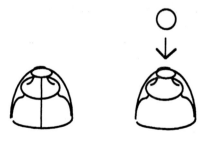

5. Cut two 3x5 squares from the light green felt and roll into tubes. Glue along the seams to secure. Glue the arms on opposite sides of the body extended outward.

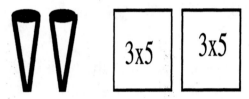

4. You can glue a small black pot of gold made from a piece of black felt in one hand.

7. Glue loopy red chenille or several wraps of red yarn to the top of the bottle cap for hair. Paint a face with black fabric paint and let dry.

6. To finish your lady leprechaun, begin at one arm and glue different colored plastic caps in an arc above her head for a rainbow.

2-LITER LARRY LEPRECHAUN

At the end of a rainbow,
his story is told.
2-liter Larry,
with pots full of gold!
A red fuzzy beard,
a full jolly grin.
A proud plastic belly
for coins to fit in.
Extending his arms
to grant every wish,
A buckle down vest,
a round plastic dish,
A black buckle hat,
that's green at the rim,
A 2-liter leprechaun,
Larry, that's him!

TO MAKE THIS CRAFT YOU NEED

1   Two- liter plastic skirt shaped bottle
2   large (milk or O.J.) plastic bottle
    caps
2   squares of green felt
1   square of white felt
Orange loopy chenille (for a beard)
Yellow fabric paint
Black fabric paint
Low melt glue gun
adult supervision

TO BEGIN

1. Cut the plastic bottle in half at
    the skirt shaped seam. Also cut
    the round plastic dish from the
    bottom of the bottle.

plastic bottle caps

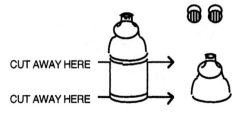

CUT AWAY HERE

CUT AWAY HERE

2. Glue the two bottle caps together
    with Tacky Glue and set aside to
    dry.

plastic bottle caps

Glue Bottle caps together

3. Cut a 12x 5 inch strip of green
    felt. Starting at the back of the
    bottle, glue the felt to the bottle
    edge bottom until you reach
    the opposite side.

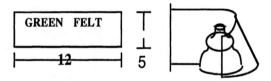

GREEN FELT

12

5

4. Glue the felt at the rim all
    around.

5. Glue the dried caps to the top of
    the bottle facing forward to
    form the head.

6. Glue loopy chenille from one
    side of the cap to the opposite
    side for hair. Glue an additional
    piece across the front for the
    beard

31

8. Cut a square of green felt 2x4 and a 2 inch circle. Fold the square in half and glue it shut. Glue the square in the center of the circle to form the hat.

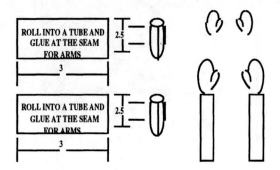

9. Paint a yellow strip across the bottom of the square with yellow fabric paint. LET DRY. When dry, paint a black square on top of the yellow to form a buckle.

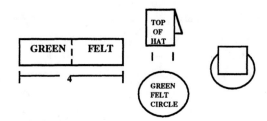

10. Glue the hat to the top of the head.

11. Cut two 3x2.5 inch squares of green felt, roll each of them into a tight tube and glue shut at the seams. Cut two small mittens from the white felt and glue each one to the top of the green tubes for arms.

12. Glue the arms to the back of the bottle and extend the hands outstreched.

13. Paint a yellow vest on the front of the doll with yellow fabric paint. When dry, outline the vest in black and paint buttons along the front seam.

HIDE SHINY COINS BELOW THE BOTTLE!

32

BOTTLE CAP
CLASSROOM CLOVERS

Save your green plastic lids!
We're making clovers for kids.
The leprechauns want some too!
Now let's show them what to do!

TO MAKE THIS CRAFT YOU NEED

3 green plastic bottle caps per child
1 green chenille stem per child
Tacky Glue
Green glitter
1 photo of each child
Low melt glue gun   (adult supervision)
1 square of green felt per child
scissors

TO BEGIN

1. Cut each photograph the diameter of the inside of 1 cap.

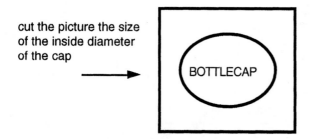

cut the picture the size
of the inside diameter
of the cap

BOTTLECAP

2. Fill the inside of the cap with a thin layer of Tacky glue and press the picture in place to secure.   (set aside)

3. Cut three strips of green felt the same width of the side diameter of each cap. Use the glue gun to secure the felt in place.

Glue each cap to each other with the photograph inside the top cap.

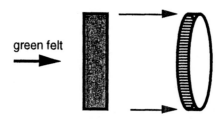

green felt

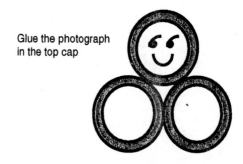

Glue the photograph
in the top cap

4. Use the gluegun to secure a chenille stem on that flat back of each clover

5. Place Tacky glue around the rim of each cap and smash the clover into green glitter to frame the picture and make the clover board and cap off the class!

NOTES

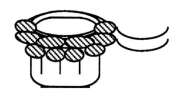

APRIL

BOTTLE CAP BASKET

TO MAKE THIS CRAFT YOU NEED

1   plastic fabric softener cup cap
1   chenille stem (your choice of color)
Gathered lace or flat
(your choice of color)
Low melt glue gun with adult
supervision
Green Easter grass

TO BEGIN

1. Glue gathered lace just under the rim all around the cup, or press the wide end of decorative flat ribbon into warm glue below the rim.

2. Make a chain of loops around the cap connecting each loop with glue.

3. Cut a chenille stem to the desired length to for the handle. Dress up the handle by wrapping metallic bead cord or ribbon around the stem and securing it at both ends with glue.

4. Place a dab of glue inside one of the ribbon loops on the outside of the cap. Glue and conceal it within the loop. (Repeat for the opposite side)

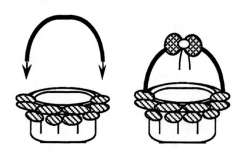

5. Attach a bow or ribbon or seasonal miniature to the center of the handle. Fill your basket with green grass and goodies!

BABY BOTTLE CAP BUNNY

A bottle cap bunny that wears a lace
bonnet,
A bead for a face with whiskers upon it,
With Q-tip arms glue
tight into place,
Wearing a skirt with
lace at the base.
Fit for a pencil, a cupcake or toy,
Easter fun for a girl or a boy.

TO MAKE THIS CRAFT YOU NEED

1   dishwashing liquid push-pull top
1   16mm wooden bead face
Gathered lace (color of your choice)
2   Q-tips

TO BEGIN

1.   Separate the top half from the
bottom of your push-pull top.
Save the top part for another
craft in this book. For this craft,
we need only the bottom portion
of this top.

(set aside)

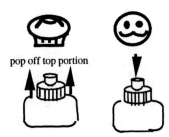

pop off top portion

2.   Glue lace around the wooden
bead to form an Easter
bonnet. Glue the bead to the
top of the lid at the stem.

Glue gathered lace around
the neck to form a collar.

3.   Cut one Q-tip in half and
glue them to the back of the
bead to form bunny ears.

4.   Cut the other Q-tip in half
and glue each to the stem
on each side to form arms.

5.   Glue gathered lace around
the bottom for a skirt.
Repeat rows and layers for
a full effect.

6.   Paint a bunny face from
the model shown or
draw your own.
LET DRY.

7.   You can glue this bunny to
the top of a pencil, or set
her in the middle of a
cupcake, or trim an easter
basket with her!

Cut in half here---

BOTTLE CAP CROSS

Glue four bottle caps
  in a line,
  in a row.
With one on each side,
And a cross soon will show.
  Embellish the hollows,
  With roses or trim
To enhance any holiday,
  Honoring him.

TO MAKE THIS CRAFT YOU NEED

6 matching 2 liter plastic bottle caps
Tacky Glue
Glitter (Color of choice)
1 Skein of metallic bead cord
(color of choice)
Q-tips
4 Ribbon Roses
Low melt glue gun
adult supervision

TO BEGIN

1. Glue the clean and dried caps
    together with a low melt glue
    gun to form across with the
    hollows facing forward.

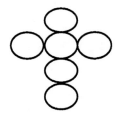

2. Spread Tacky Glue across
    the top and sides of the
    entire cross.

3. Press the end of the
    metallic bead cord into the
    back edge of the top cap.
    Hold in place a few
    seconds until set

4. Begin rotating the cord
    around the entire cross.

5. Press the cord into each
    corner with a Q-tip or a
    pencil and hold in place a
    few seconds until set.
    Continue wrapping the
    cord until you reach the
    middle of the top cap.

STOP

6. Make a six inch loop and tie a slip knot at the bottom of the loop.

   (JUST LIKE TYING YOUR SHOE!)

7. Pull tightly on the cord to shrink and center the knot.

8. Continue rotating the cord until the entire surface of each cap is covered.

9. Snip the cord with scissors and secure in place with glue.

10. Place a generous amount of Tacky Glue within the hollow of each cap. Swirl it around with a Q-tip until all exposed areas of the bottom and sides are covered.

11. Fill each cap with glitter up to the rim. Turn each cap over a folded piece of paper and tap the bottle cap back to catch the excess.
   LET DRY

12. Glue a ribbon rose into each of the center hollows.

13. Cover the knot at the top by gluing a rose or a bow to it. You can glue a strand of beaded pearls around the cross to embellish.

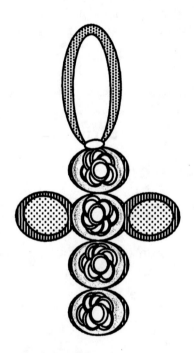

14. Glue family pictures into the hollows for a unique gift!

BOTTLE CAP BUNNY BOTTLE

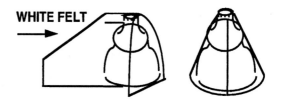

WHITE FELT

Bottle cap bunnies are fluffy and white,
Their whiskers are made from chenille.
They hop in your baskets in colors so bright,
And they're soft and so cuddly to feel!
With pom pom tails and felt pointed ears,
    Glued to the back of a lid,
They'll be a treasure for many years,
    Just look in the eyes of a kid!

TO MAKE THIS CRAFT YOU NEED:

1 Two liter plastic bottle
2 white round plastic milk caps
5 pink pom poms
1 square of white felt
1 square of pink felt
Tacky Glue
Pink Fabric Paint
Wiggle eyes

TO BEGIN

1. Carefully cut the two liter bottle
    in half at the seam. Set aside.
    Glue the plastic caps together with
    tacky glue and let dry.

(ADULT SUPERVISION REQUIRED)

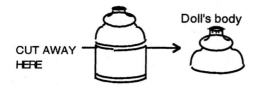

CUT AWAY HERE

Doll's body

2. Cover the body with white felt
    and secure at the seam in the back
    with a low melt glue gun.

3. Glue the dried bottle caps to
    the top of the body for the
    head.

4. Cut a small oval from the
    pink felt and glue to the
    tummy below the head.
    Glue small pink pom poms
    on each side of the body for
    arms and legs. Don't
    for get the tail in the back!

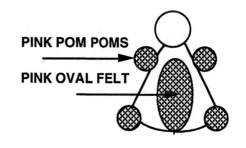

PINK POM POMS

PINK OVAL FELT

5. Cut two ears from white felt and cut two small pink ovals to glue in the center. Glue the ears to the back of the bottle cap head.

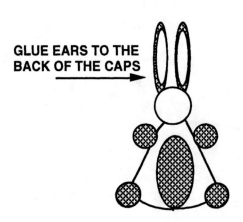

**GLUE EARS TO THE
BACK OF THE CAPS**

6. Glue chenille stems to the face for whiskers. Glue on wiggle eyes and paint a smile cheeks and nose with pink fabric paint.

Hide Goodies Underneath!

MAY

BOTTLE CAP CORSAGE
TO MAKE THIS CRAFT YOU NEED
1 plastic bottle cap
Tacky Glue
Crystal   glitter
1 ft of lace (any type)
low melt glue gun
6 inched of beaded pearl strand
YOUR PICTURE
Modge Podge

TO BEGIN
1. Wash and dry the plastic cap.
   Turn it over on top of a paper
   towel and leave until all moisture
   inside the cap is dry.

BOTTLE CAP

2. Use the glue gun to pleat the lace
   against the flat back of the cap all
   the way around until the edges of
   the lace along the (open-edge) seam
   with the glue gun.

GLUE LACE TO THE FLAT
BACK OF THE CAP
PLEATING AS YOU GO

BOTTLE CAP

3. Use the glue gun to glue a
   beaded pearl strand around the
   diameter of the cap on top of
   the lace. Snip it at the end and
   secure in place with glue.

4. To finish the coursage, glue a
   photocopy of your favorite
   picture into the center of the
   bottle cap. Preserve it by
   brushing Modge Podge on top of
   it and let it dry overnight.

5. Glue a peel back pin to the back
   of the corsage so mom can pin it
   on her!

41

NOTES

POP TOP PICTURE FRAME

By gluing four caps in a row, at the top,
Four on each side,
and bottom, then stop.
Balance each side, to measure the
same,
The right combination, for making a
frame.
Fill every hollow with glitter and glue,
Embellish with roses, a bouquet or two.
Insert your best picture,
or drawing or poem,
And give as a gift ,
to be hung in your home!

TO MAKE THIS CRAFT YOU NEED

12 plastic 2 liter bottle caps
A 4x4 cardboard cut from a cereal box
1 skein of metallic bead cord
Tacky Glue
Q-tips
Glitter (any color you like)
Low melt glue gun with adult
supervision

TO BEGIN

1. Place a generous amount of Tacky Glue within the hollow of each cap. Swirl it around until all exposed areas of the sides and bottom are covered.

2. Fill each cap with glitter up to the rim. Turn each cap over a folded piece of paper and tap the bottle cap back to recover the excess glitter.
LET DRY

3. Once dry, use the low melt glue gun to glue 4 bottle caps side by side.

GLUE 4 CAPS SIDE BY SIDE

4. Glue 3 more caps down the side from each corner.

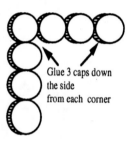
Glue 3 caps down the side from each corner

5. Close off the frame by gluing the last two caps across the bottom.

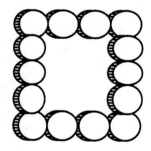

6. Cut the back panel of a cereal box into a 4x4 square. Glue the panel to the flat side of the caps.

Glue a 4x4 cereal box panel to the back of the bottle caps

7. Spread tacky glue around the entire side surface of the pop-top frame.

8. Press the end of metallic bead cord into the corner cap at the edge. Begin rotating the cord until you reach the center at the top of the frame.

STOP

9. Make a six inch loop and tie a simple slip knot at the bottom of the loop. Pull tightly on the cord to shrink and center the knot.

10. Continue rotating until you've covered the entire frame. Snip at the end and secure in place with glue.

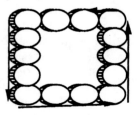

11. Glue a bow or ribbon rose to the knot to embellish. Fill the hollows with stickers, flowers or minatures.

12. Slip your best picture through the bottom. Give as a gift to grandma or mom!

JUNE

BIRDCAGE PAPERWEIGHT

IF WE LOOK TO THE SKY,
AND THE CREATURES THAT FLY,
WE'LL SEE THEIR RESPECT
FOR THE PLANET,
THEY TAKE WHAT THEY NEED,
FOR SHELTER AND FEED,
WITHOUT TAKING ONE THING
FOR GRANTED.
WITH SOME CORD AND TWO CAPS,
SOME GLITTER PERHAPS,
IN INTERVALS WITH SOFT CHENILLE,
A TINY BIRD PLACED,
EMBELLISHED WITH LACE,
CREATES A BIRDCAGE SO REAL!

TO MAKE THIS CRAFT YOU NEED

2 matching plastic milk bottle caps
A miniature toy craft bird
3 chenille stems (any color)
Ribbon (optional)
1 shiny bead
Low melt glue gun with adult
supervision
Scraps of lace
Tacky Glue
Sand

TO BEGIN

1   Fill the hollow of one milk cap
    with sand. Place Tacky glue
    around the rim and glue
    the matching cap on top of it.
    LET DRY

plastic bottle caps

 Glue Bottle caps together

2. Glue the toy bird miniature
    in the center of the top cap
    using the low melt glue gun.

3. Bend three chenille stems
    and cut them in half.

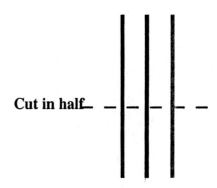

Cut in half

4. Place a dab of warm glue
    at the bottom of the first
    one. Wrap ribbon, metallic
    cord or yarn candy-cane
    fashion around the stem
    until you reach the opposite
    side.

Wrap ribbon around each stem

ALL SIX STEMS

7. Embellish the top of the cage by gluing a shiny bead to the top.

5. Bend the first stem into an arc. Glue one end at the edge of the cap. Arch across the top of the bird and glue to the opposite side. Criss-cross stems across the caps at different intervals to form the cage.

8. Present this paperweight to your favorite grandpa, uncle or dad!

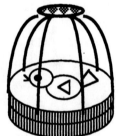

6. Glue gathered lace around the caps at the surface edge.

BOTTLE CAP DRUMS

TO MAKE THIS CRAFT YOU NEED
1 cardboard tissue roll
2 plastic milk caps (same size and color)
1 Piece of yarn
Small beads
Low melt glue gun
1 large eye sewing needle
Scissors

TO BEGIN

1. Pierce a small hole in the center of a cap.

2. Thread the yarn through the large eye needle and tie a large knot at the end.

3. Come up through the bottom of the bottle cap with the needle. Pull the yarn through the hole until the knot is set firm against the inside of the cap.

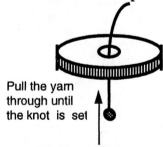

Pull the yarn through until the knot is set

4. Glue the tube inside the rim of the second plastic cap. If your tube doesn't fit the cap, cut it along the seam, make it smaller and glue in place.

glue the top cap to the top of the tube!

5. Fill the matching cap with small beads or rice and glue to the bottom of the tube.

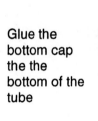
Glue the bottom cap the the bottom of the tube

6. Now decorate your drum by using markers, crayons, paint and stickers, glue or glitter! Be creative!

7. Once your decorations have dried, slip your fingers through the loop and shake the drum to the beat of your favorite song!!!

BOTTLE GRADUATION CAPS

As school draws to it's yearly end.
emotions run so high.
For everyone became a friend.
It's hard to say goodbye.
Teachers who have meant so much,
who brought their grace
and special touch,
to every child as they pass.
into their next grade or class.
But tiny tokens can be made,
to reflect on every grade,
with bottle graduation caps,
to use as keepsakes or perhaps,
to acknowledge all the kids,
by capturing them all in lids!

TO MAKE THIS CRAFT YOU NEED

Cardboard Cereal boxes folded flat
Felt (school colors preferable)
Plastic Bottle Caps (1 per student)
(Color to match school colors)
Tacky Glue
Black Fabric paint
Yarn
Glitter
School pictures (1 per student)
Low melt glue gun
adult supersvision

TO BEGIN

1. Cut cardboard squares from the
    cereal boxes into 4 by 4 inches.

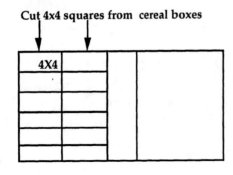

Cut 4x4 squares from cereal boxes

2. Use the glue gun to glue a
    plastic cap directly in the
    center of each card board
    square.

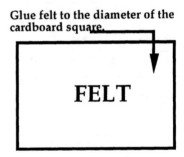

Glue bottle cap in the middle of each square

3. Glue a piece of felt to the top
    of the carboard square.
    (school colors)

Glue felt to the diameter of the cardboard square.

FELT

4. Cut several strands of yarns
    into 1 inch strips. Gather
    them together and glue at the
    end to form a tassle.

Gather the yarn in
a bunch and glue at
the end

5. Glue a long piece of yarn to the tassle and then glue the straight end to the edge of the cardboard square. Let the tassle hang down.

6. Cut each photograph just under the diameter of each bottle cap. Use tacky glue to secure each photograph in place in the center of each cap. To highlight each picture, put tacky glue around the diameter of each bottle cap and dip the entire cap in glitter. Shake of the excess.

7. Use black fabric to paint the name of each student as well as the school name on the cardboard back of each cap.

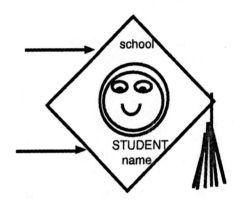

8. Glue each cap to a large bullentin board to show off the class or glue a rubber band to the back of each one and roll a graduation certificate into a tube and attach the graduation cap to each paper for presentation!

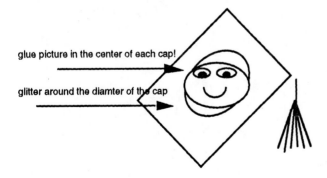

glue picture in the center of each cap!

glitter around the diamter of the cap

BOTTLE CAP KLAIDESCOPE

Cut away the cente
leave the rim

TO MAKE THIS CRAFT YOU NEED

Tacky glue
1 cardboard tissue roll
2 flexible plastic milk caps
(same size and color)
3 Strips of high polished aluminum
or highly reflective foil
Bits of multi-colored confetti
1 transparent laundry scoop
Low melt glue gun
scissors

3. Trace the diameter of the cap
   on each side of a transparent
   laundry scoop. Carefully cut
   away each circle.

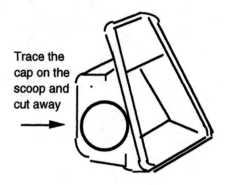

Trace the
cap on the
scoop and
cut away →

TO BEGIN

1. Pierce a small hole in the center
    of one cap. Glue it to the end of
    the tissue tube. If your cap does
    not fit the diameter of the cap
    exactly, cut the tube in half and
    roll it back inside the bottle cap
    rim. Using the low melt glue gun,
    glue the tube inside the rim
    diameter of the bottle cap.

4. Use tacky glue to glue a
   transparent circle inside the
   bottle cap rim.
   Let   Dry

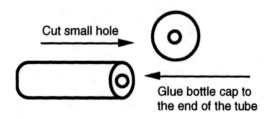

Cut small hole →

← Glue bottle cap to
the end of the tube

5. Fill the cap with brightly
    colored confetti, foil or small
    beads. Allow enough space for
    the confetti to move freely and
    glue the second transprent
    circle on top.

2.   Cut the flat circle away from the
      top of the second cap. Leave the
      rim intact.

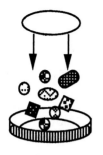

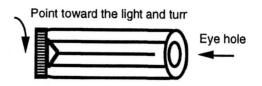

Point toward the light and turr

Eye hole

6. Cut three strips of highly polished foil 1/2 inch wide and equal in length to the length of the tube. Glue the strip along the seams to form a triangle.

10. Once everything is in place, decorate the tube by painting, tracing stencils, using stickers or covering with wrapping paper. Give as a delightful gift or make one for yourself!

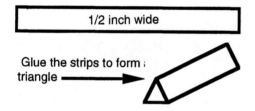

1/2 inch wide

Glue the strips to form triangle ➜

7. Once the triangle is set and dry. Fit the Cap with confetti on the open end of the tube. Do not glue this cap so that it may turn. Point the tube toward a light. Look through the small eye hole while turning the cap at the end. You should see many remarkable designs.

See the world in a whole new light!

RECYCLED ROBOT

Robbie the Robot has a bottle cap head,
His body's a paper towel roll.
His arms will extend, fold down and bend,
and *buttons* will give him control!
His feet will roll on bottle cap wheels,
To make him can be so much fun!
So make more than two,
it's all up to you,
but you'll never stop at just one!

TO MAKE THIS CRAFT YOU NEED

white matching plastic bottle caps
(milk or O.J size)
1 paper towel roll
1 square of grey or yellow felt
a variety of buttons and sequins
Fabric paint
Tacky Glue
Low melt glue gun with (adult
supervision)
2 chenille stems
2 push-pull tops

TO BEGIN

1. Glue two of the white caps
    together with Tacky glue and
    set aside to dry.

plastic bottle caps

  Glue Bottle caps together

2. Use the glue gun to glue felt
    to the paper towel roll.

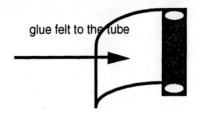
glue felt to the tube

3. Glue bottle caps to the top
    of the tube to form the robot
    head.

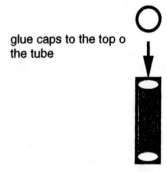
glue caps to the top o
the tube

4. Glue 1 cap to the bottom of
    the tube to balance the body.

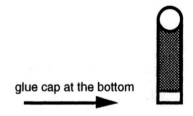
glue cap at the bottom

5. Poke a hole through the
    center of two of the
    remaining caps. Gently
    poke a hole 1/2 inch below
    the bottle cap head and
    another hole just above the
    bottom cap.

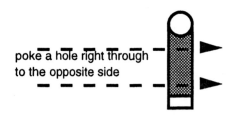

poke a hole right through
to the opposite side

8. Glue buttons or sequins
down the front for a
control panel.

6. Push the first chenille stem through
the top hole and the second through
the bottom. Push the bottle caps
with holes onto the chenille stems
at the bottom and twist the excess
stem into a loose knot so that the
wheels turn.

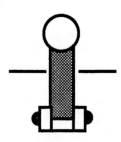

7. Glue push-pull tops to each
chenille stems for arms.

9. Use fabric paint to design
a robot face for Robbie or
glue your own picture to
the cap!

Glue push-pull tops the
sides for arms.

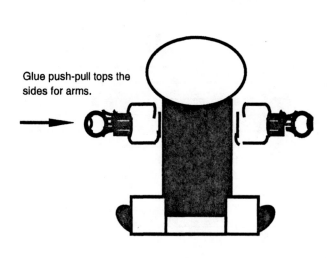

NOTES

JULY
BOTTLE CAP CLOWN

It's the 4th of July!
It's red, white and blue.
A hot air balloon
and a yo-yo or two,
Will enhance any party,
and erase any frown.
Bring cheer to the crowd
with a bottle cap clown!

TO MAKE THIS CRAFT YOU NEED

1 two liter plastic skirt shaped bottle
2 matching plastic white bottle caps
The bottom half of a dishwashing liquid
(push-pull top)
3 blue transparent bottle cap liners
Orange or red loopy chenille
Needle and white thread
Black and red Fabric paint
3 red chenille stems
1.5 yards of polka dot clown fabric
4 large red pom-poms
4 medium red pom poms
Low melt glue gun
adult supervision
Tacky glue

TO BEGIN

1. Cut the 2 liter bottle in half at the skirt indention. Use the bottom half of the bottle to collect your scraps of fabric. This craft requires only the top skirt shaped portion.

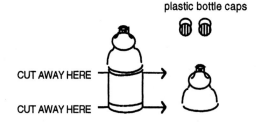

plastic bottle caps

CUT AWAY HERE

CUT AWAY HERE

2. Glue your bottle caps together with Tacky Glue and set aside to dry.

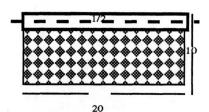

plastic bottle caps

Glue Bottle caps together

3. Cut a square of fabric that measures 10 x 20 inches and fold down the top edge 1/2

inch.

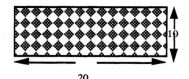

4. Sew a simple hem stitch along the fold and gently pull the thread to gather the material. This will form the clown collar. Glue the gathered collar around the neck of the bottle using the low melt glue gun.

55

5. Cut the fabric up from the bottom 10 inches. This will form the leg holes. Fold the fabric 1/2 inch at the bottom of each leg.

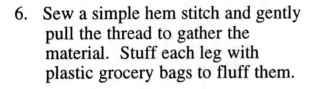

6. Sew a simple hem stitch and gently pull the thread to gather the material. Stuff each leg with plastic grocery bags to fluff them.

7. Glue the legs shut at the seams. Glue 3 red medium pom-poms to the front of the clown suit for buttons.

8. Glue 2 large red pom-poms at the bottom of each leg for shoes.

9. Cut a square of fabric that measures 10x6. Cut that same square in half. Sew a simple hem stitch and gently pull on the thread to gather the material. Tie and cut the thread.

10. Stuff the arms with scraps of plastic grocery bags to fluff them. Glue the straight sides of the arms below the clown collar at the back of the bottle.

11. Glue a red pom-pom at the end of each arm to form hands.

12. Using the glue gun, glue the dried bottle caps to the top of the bottle facing forward.

13. Glue loopy red chenille from one end of the bottle caps to the opposite side to form hair.

14. Glue 3 red chenille stems into the pom-pom hand on one side. Glue 3 blue or white bottle cap liners to the top of each stem to form balloons.

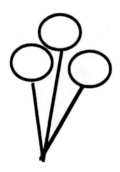

15. Glue the bottom half of a push-pull dishwashing liquid top to the top of his head for a hat. Embellish the hat with a red pom-pom or a small flower.

16. Using Fabric paint, paint a clown face from the model shown or use your imagination to paint your own clown face!

YOUR CLOWN WILL SIT NEATLY ON YOUR DRESSER, OR SLIP YOUR HAND INSIDE THE BOTTLE AND USE HIM AS A PUPPET!

HOT AIR EGGSHELL BALLOON
TO MAKE THIS CRAFT YOU NEED:

1   blown out clean and dried eggshell
1   plastic bottle cap that measures
1/2 inch wide and 1/2 inch deep
(caps of choice are found on hair care
products, dentures cremes and
toothpaste)
4   chenille stems
1   skien of metallic bead cord
       (Your choice of color)
A dishwashing liquid push-pull top
Tacky Glue
Low melt glue gun with adult
supervision

TO BEGIN

1. (Instructions for blowing out
    your eggshell can be found on
    the craft collection pages
    at the begining of this book.)

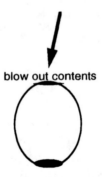

blow out contents

2. Place a 1/2 inch line of Tacky
   Glue around the circumference
   of the eggshell.

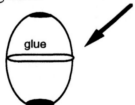

glue

3. Pick up metallic bead cord
   and begin rotating it
   around the eggshell
   creating rows to cover the
   seam surface. Snip with a
   scissors and secure in
   place with glue.

4. Apply a second line of
   tacky glue vertically
   across the eggshell
   covering the cord already
   in place. Wrap metallic
   cord around the
   circumference of the shell
   covering the cord
   already in place.

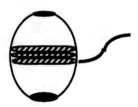

5. Cut 4 chenille stems in
   half. Embellish your stems
   by wrapping cord or
   ribbon around each one.
   Secure in place with glue
   at the end.

   (Repeat this procedure for stems)

58

6. Place 4 dabs of glue on top of the vertical cord spacing each at 2 cm intervals. Press a chenille stem into each dab and hold in place until set. Repeat the same procedure on the opposite side of the egg with the remaining stems.

8. Gather the first 4 stems into a point and glue to the inside of the bottle cap.

9. Repeat this procedure on the opposite side.

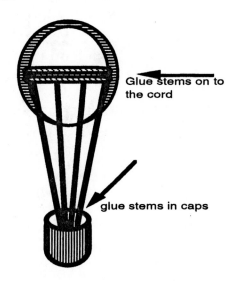

Glue stems on to the cord

glue stems in caps

10. Use the glue gun to glue the top portion of a dishwashing liquid top to the tip of the balloon on top of the cord.

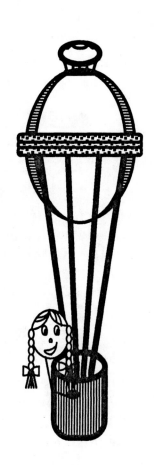

BOTTLE CAP YO-YO

TO MAKE THIS CRAFT YOU NEED

2 plastic bottle caps that measure
3.5mm wide (same size shape and
color)
2 plastic milk or O.J. caps
(same shape and color)
1 1/2 inch wooden spool
24" thin cotton twine
Low Melt glue gun
adult supervision
Fabric paints or stickers (optional)
Tacky Glue

TO BEGIN

Two 3.5mm wide plastic caps

Two plastic milk or O.J. caps

1. Using an exacto knife, carefully
cut away a 5/8 inch hole from
the center of your milk or O.J.
caps

Cut away the middle
circle of both milk caps

2. Using the glue gun, glue the end
of the twine to the center of your
wooden spool. Wrap around
a few times to secure.

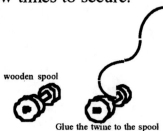

wooden spool

Glue the twine to the spool

3. Push the wooden spool
through the hole of each
milk cap. Secure in place
with the glue gun. Push the
caps so that they are close
but not touching.

Glue the milk caps to each side of the
wooden spool

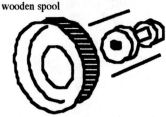

4. Spread a generous amount
of Tacky Glue inside the
rim of the larger caps.
Press the larger caps on
top of the smaller ones.
Push until the two caps are
set flush against each other.

LET DRY

5. Paint, sticker or glitter the
flat bottle cap faces! Tie
the loose end of the twine
into a loop for your finger.

AUGUST

BOTTLE CAP KEY CHAIN

TO MAKE THIS CRAFT YOU NEED:

2 matching plastic bottle caps
1 Key ring
Metallic bead cord
Tacky Glue

TO BEGIN

1. Glue the bottle caps together
   with Tacky glue and let dry.

plastic bottle caps

  Glue Bottle caps together

2. Spread Tacky glue along the
   entire seam side surface and
   rub well into the grooves with
   your finger.
   (Wipe your finger dry before
   proceeding)

3. Press metallic bead cord into
   the edge of the caps at the rim.
   Begin rotating the cord around
   the cap until you reach the middle
   of the two caps. **STOP HERE**

4. Make a 6 inch loop with
   the cord and tie a slip knot
   at the base of the loop.
   Pull tightly on the cord to
   shrink and center the knot.

5. Continue rotating the cord
   around the cap until you've
   covered the entire exposed
   side surface.

6. Snip the cord and secure in
   place with glue. Slip a key
   ring on the loop.

7. Paint, sticker, glitter or
   glue your favorite
   picture to each side of
   your bottle cap key chain.

BOTTLE CAP BOOKMARK

TO MAKE THIS CRAFT YOU NEED

1   popsicle stick
1   white liner found inside milkcaps
Yarn (any favorite color)
Low melt glue gun with adult
supervision
Tacky Glue

TO BEGIN

1. Glue the end of the yarn to the
    tip of the popsicle stick. Wrap
    the yarn around the stick until
    the entire surface of the stick is
    covered. Secure at the bottom
    with glue.

2. Glue the white liner to the top of
    the stick. Tacky glue your favorite
    picture, sticker or photograph to
    the center of the liner.

3. Embellish the liner with glitter
    around the center picture.

4. Use as a bookmark or give as gift
    to someone very special!

SEPTEMBER

PATCHES
THE PLASTIC SCARECROW

Patches was born with a bottle cap head,
Covered in plastic
from a warm loaf of bread.
Dressed in green felt with a patch on his coat
A chenille stem is twisted
around his wide throat.
He's wearing white gloves
for scaring the birds,
He does it with silence without any words.
Even his hat has a little square patch,
His painted on eyes don't really match,
But Patches stands tall,
he's anxious to play.
Recycle your bottles and do it today!

TO MAKE THIS CRAFT YOU NEED

1   plastic 2 liter skirt shaped bottle
2   matching plastic bottle caps
1   brown plastic grocery bag
1   black chenille stem
1   yard of green felt
1   square of white felt
1   square of black felt
1   miniature bird
Orange Fabric paint
Black Fabric paint
White Fabric paint
Blue Fabric Paint
Tacky Glue
Low melt glue gun
 adult supervision
Orange Yarn

TO BEGIN

1. Cut the 2 liter bottle in half at the skirt indention. Use the bottom half of the bottle to collect your scraps o fabric. This craft requires only the top skirt shaped portion.

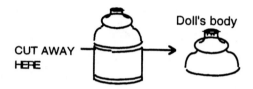

CUT AWAY HERE → Doll's body

2. Glue your bottle caps together with Tacky glue and set aside to dry.

plastic bottle caps

  Glue Bottle caps together

3. Glue the dried caps to the top of the bottle with the low melt glue gun to form the head.

plastic bag

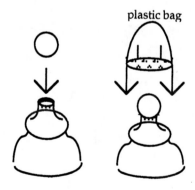

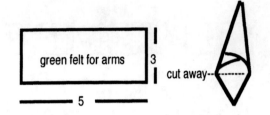

4. Cut the brown plastic bag into a 3x5 square. Wrap tightly around the bottle caps to form the wrinkled face. Twist the black chenille stem around the neck to | form the black tie.

5. Starting at the back of the bottle, wrap green felt below the plastic collar around the bottle. Secure in place with the glue gun at the back.

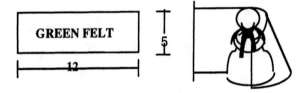

6. Glue a strip of black felt around the waist to form the belt.

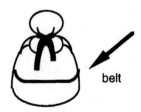

belt

7. Fold two 3x5 inch pieces of green felt squares into cones and glue at the seams.

green felt for arms   3

cut away--

5

8. Cut 2 small white gloves from the white felt and glue with the glue gun at the end of the sleeve cones.

9. Glue the arms to the back of the bottle underneath the plastic collar be sure that the arms are extended outward.

10. Glue small orange squares to the body for patches.

11. To make the hat, cut a 3x5 inch square of green felt and a 3.5 inch circle of green felt. Fold the square into a cone and glue at the seam. Glue the cone to the center of the circle.

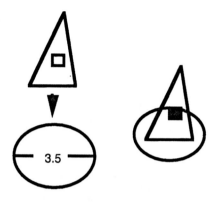

12. Glue orange yarn to the top of the head and fluff for hair. Glue the green hat on top of the yarn.

13. Paint a face with fabric paint following the model shown or use your imagination and paint your own.   LET DRY.

14. Glue a miniature bird to his extended arm.

PAPER BAG INDIAN PRINCESS

Long black shiny hair, that falls to her feet,
This Indian princess is really quite sweet.
Her paper bag poncho
and sleeves from the pieces,
Are shaped when you fold and
You press out the creases.
Now zig-zag the paint
and trim up the base,
Carefully paint a sweet Indian face,
Make a papoose and glue in her hands,
Embellish the collar,
make feathers from plastic,
Recycle your scraps
to make something fantastic!

TO MAKE THIS CRAFT YOU NEED

1   2 liter plastic skirt shaped bottle
2   matching plastic bottle caps
4   yellow garbage bag twist ties
1   brown paper lunch bag
1   16mm painted bead face
Tacky glue
 Low Melt Glue Gun
adult supervision
Variety of Fabric Paints

TO BEGIN

1. Cut the 2 liter bottle in half at the
    skirt indention. Use the bottom
    half of the bottle to collect your
    scraps of fabric. This craft
    requires only the top skirt shaped
    portion.

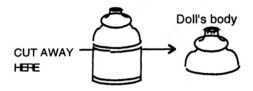

CUT AWAY HERE   Doll's body

2. Glue your bottle caps
    together with Tacky glue
    and set aside to dry.

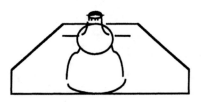

plastic bottle caps   Glue Bottle caps together

3. Open a brown paper lunch
    bag at the seams. Press out
    the bag with your hand
    into a large square. Fold
    down the top of the bag
    1/2 inch.

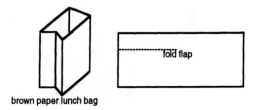

fold flap

brown paper lunch bag

4. Wrap the corners around
    each side of the doll and
    criss-cross the bag to
    overlap at the bottom of the
    bottle.

Criss cross bag to overlap at the bottom of the bottle

5. Glue the bag in place at the
   center. Cut away the excess bag
   and set aside.

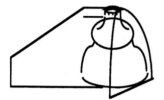

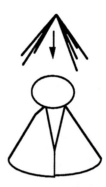

9. Glue plastic yellow garbage
   bags twist ties around the
   front of the head to form
   the headband.

6. Glue the dried bottle caps to the
   top of the bottle facing forward.

Glue bottle cap head to the body

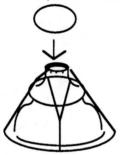

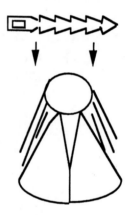

7. Fold two 3x5 paper squares into
   cones and glue at the seams.
   SET ASIDE.

10. Glue four twist ties at the
    back of the headband
    pointing upward to represent
    feathers. Paint each feather
    a bright, hot color with
    fabric paints. **LET DRY**

8. Glue black yarn or black
   embroidery floss to the top of
   the bottle cap head to
   form hair.
   (You can braid on each side if
   you like)

67

12. Glue another twist below the face at the bottle rim to form the colorful collar. Paint the collar with brightly colored fabric paints.
LET DRY

14. From the remaining paper bag pieces. Form a small cone and glue together at the seams. Glue a painted bead face at the top of the cone. Insert the papoose in between the sleeves and glue in place with the face facing forward.

13. Glue the paper bag sleeve cones in the center of the poncho on opposite side.

15. At the base of the poncho, zig-zag paints all around the bottle.   LET DRY.

16. Paint a sweet Indian face from the model shown or use your imagination and paint your own! Indian Word Symbols

**Native Americans are our first recyclers as they took nothing for granted. After visiting an Indian Retreat in New Mexico, a friend of mine passed on these word symbols to me that she had learned while she was there. Use them to draw your own symbols when you decorate the dress of your Indian Princess

Indian Word Symbol
Thunderbird-----------Happiness
Arrow------------------Protection
Arrow head----------- Allertness
Saddlebags----------- Journey
Bird--------------------Carefree
Horse---------------- Journey
Man------------------ Human Life
Lasso----------------- Captivity
Hogan-----------------Permanent Home
Tepee------------------Temporary Home
Sun Rays------------- Constancy
Deer Track------------Plenty Game
Eagle Feather --------Chief
Lightening---------- Swiftness
Bear Track--------- Good Omen
Butterfly------------- Everylasting Life
Headdress----------- Ceremonial Dance
Rain Cloud-----------Good Prospects
Day & Night---------Time
Sun Symbol---------Happiness
Big Mountain-------Abundance
Snake----------------Wisdom
Crossed Arrows-----Friendship

NOTES

OCTOBER

POP TOP PUMPKIN PENDANTS

Two bright orange caps,
and some thick
Tacky Glue,
A few feet of yarn
and some fabric paint too!
A green push pull top,
and a pattern to trace,
A wide toothy grin,
on a hot orange face.
Plucked from the trash,
instead of a patch,
Make one for yourself,
or make a whole batch!

TO MAKE THIS CRAFT YOU NEED

2 matching plastic orange bottle caps
A few feet of green yarn
A green push-pull dishwashing liquid top
Black fabric paint
Tacky Glue

TO BEGIN

1. Glue the bottle caps together with Tacky Glue and set aside to dry.

plastic bottle caps

 Glue Bottle caps together

2. Spread Tacky glue around the entire circumference of the dried caps.

3. Press the tip of the green yarn on to the outer edge of the caps. Begin rotating the yarn until you reach the center seam.
   ### STOP

4. Make an 18 inch loop with the yarn and tie a simple slip knot at the end of the loop. Pull tightly on the cord to shrink and center the knot.

5. Continue rotating until you've reached the edge. Snip with scissors and secure in place with glue.

6. Use only the green top portion of your push-pull top. Push the end of the yarn through the hole at the top of the tip. Pull the yarn through the hole until you reached the bottle caps and cover the knot. Secure in place with glue.

7. Use black Fabric paint to design a face for your pumpkin. Follow the model shown or create your own scary face. You'll be the hit of your Halloween party.

BOTTLE CAP SPIDERS

From under the trash ,
that ispiled outside,
Bottle cap spiders, just love to hide.
Select a dark blue or purple milk cap.
Bend chenille stems
and glue to the scrap.
The pieces are set
with balance and space.
Wiggle eyes glued
to a black pom-pom face.
He's sneaky and creepy
with legs you can bend!
Keep one for yourself
and give one to a friend!

2. Glue a black furry pom-pom in the center of the cap. Glue wiggle eyes to the face.

TO MAKE THIS CRAFT YOU NEED

1 dark blue or purple plastic milk cap
1 large black fuzzy pom-pom
4 black chenille stems
Wiggle eyes
Low melt glue gun with adult supervision
Scrap of black felt

TO BEGIN

1. Cut four black chenille stems in half. Bend each one into an arc. Glue them at spaced intervals inside the cap to form the spider legs.

73

BOTTLE CAP CAT

TO MAKE THIS CRAFT YOU NEED
1   dark blue or purple
     plastic bottle cap
2   black chenille stems
     Scrap of black felt
Low melt glue gun
     adult supervision
Glow in the dark Yellow Fabric Paint

TO BEGIN
1. Glue a black furry pom-pom inside the bottle cap. Cut two small triangles from felt and glue to the flat back face of the bottle cap pointing upward.

2. Bend a black chenille stem into an arc. Glue the end to the flat bottle cap back. Cut the other stem into four pieces to form the crooked tail and the legs. Glue to the arc with the glue gun.

3. Paint slanted eyes with glow-in the dark fabric paint. You can glue a pin to the back of the cap to wear the cat on your shoulder!

BOTTLE CAP BAT

TO MAKE THIS CRAFT YOU NEED:
1   dark blue or purple bottle cap
1   square of black felt
2   feet of black yarn
Low melt glue gun and Wiggle eyes

TO BEGIN:
1. Glue a black furry pom-pom to the inside of the bottle cap. Spread Tacky glue around the outside rim surface of the bottle cap. Press yarn into the glue at the edge. Begin rotating the yarn around the diameter. Stop when you reach the center.

2. Make an 18 inch loop and tie a simple slip knot at the base of the loop. Continue rotating the yarn until you reach the edge of the cap. Cut with a scissors and secure in place with glue.

3. Cut 2 black bat wings from the black felt square. Glue to the flat back of the cap on each side. Glue wiggle eyes to the pom pom.

PLASTIC POLTERGEIST

To top off the flashlights
on Halloween night,
This plastic poltergeist
gives you a fright!
Wrapped in the wax
from cereal boxes,
He wards off the witches
and spirits and foxes.
Transparent in form
with a bottle cap head,
He lights up the way
on the night of the dead!

TO MAKE THIS CRAFT YOU NEED

1 2 liter skirt shaped plastic bottle
2 white plastic matching bottle caps
1 cereal box waxed paper
1 black chenille stem
Black Fabric paint
Tacky glue

TO BEGIN

1. Cut the 2 liter bottle in half at the
   skirt indention. Use the bottom
   half of the bottle to collect your
   scraps of fabric. This craft
   requires only the top skirt shaped
   portion.

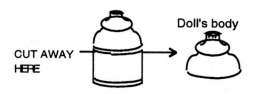

2. Glue your bottle caps together
   with Tacky glue and set aside
   to dry.

plastic bottle caps

 Glue Bottle caps together

3. Glue the dried caps to the top
   of the bottle facing forward.

4. Wrap the wax paper from a
   cereal box around the head of
   the poltergeist. Leave the
   excess wax paper hangin
   down.

5. Tie a black chenille stem
   tightly around the throat.

6. Use black fabric paint to paint
   a scary face.
                   LET DRY.

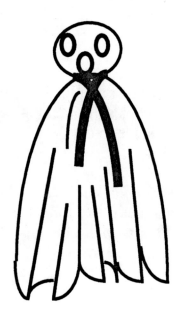

BOTTLE CAP
COUNT DRACULA

TO MAKE THIS CRAFT YOU NEED

1 Two liter plastic bottle
2 white round plastic bottle caps
2 large squares of black felt
1 square of white felt
1 small red bow tie
Black Fabric Paint
Tacky Glue
2 yellow plast garbage bag twist ties
Low melt glue gun

TO BEGIN

1. Carefully cut the two liter bottle in half at the middle.

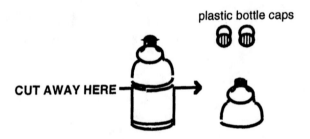

2. Glue the two plastic bottle caps together with tacky glue and set aside to dry.

3. Wrap black felt around the body and cut it to fit the shape. Using the low melt glue gun, glue at the middle seam.

4. Glue the dried caps to the top of the bottle.

5. Cut a long piece of black at an angle to for the cap. Measure from the top of the bottle to the base and make the cape as wide as you like. Cut a high collar and glue it behind the head at the top of the cape.

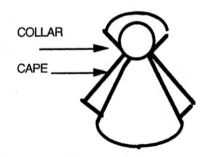

76

6. To make arms for the count. Roll two small equal squares into a tube and glue at the seams. Cut two white circles from a scrap of white felt and glue to the end of each tube.

7. Glue the arms to each side of the body. Cut a piece of white felt that measures from the neck of the bottle to the base.
Cut it to fit the pattern shown or any width you like. Glue it to the front of the body below the neck and glue it to the base as well.

White Felt Vest

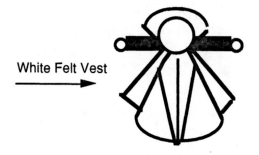

8. Glue a small red bow tie below the neck. Paint the top of his head black with fabric paint. Cut the tips off of twist ties and glue it to his face for fangs. Paint straight lines across his face for eyes!

Fangs a lot!

TWO LITER
TABLETOP TERROR

TO MAKE THIS CRAFT YOU NEED
1 plastic 2 liter skirt shaped bottle
2 plastic matching orange bottle caps
1 brown plastic grocery bag
1 black plastic garbage bag
1 square of black felt
1 straw
Orange colored yarn
Tacky glue
Low melt glue gun
adult supervision
Black fabric paint

TO BEGIN

1. Cut the 2 liter bottle in half at the skirt indention. Use the bottom half of the bottle to collect your scraps of fabric. This craft requires only the top skirt shaped portion.

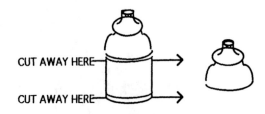

CUT AWAY HERE

CUT AWAY HERE

2. Glue your bottle caps together with Tacky glue and set aside to dry.

plastic bottle caps

  Glue Bottle caps together

3. Glue the dried bottle caps to the top of the bottle facing forward. Glue the black garbage around the bottle below the head to make the witch dress. Let the excess hang down.

4. Glue strands of orange yarn to the top of the head for hair. Cut a 3.5 inch circle from black felt and a 3.5 inch square. Roll the square into a cone and glue at the seam. Glue the cone to the center of the circle and then glue the hat to the top of the head.

5. Roll 2 more squares that measure 3.5 inches. Roll into a tube and glue at the seams to form the sleeves. Glue on opposite sides of the bottle for arms.

6. Glue brown yarn to the straw and wrap around until it is completely covered. Glue at the end. Stuff the bendable part of the straw with shredded pieces of a brown plastic grocery bag. Glue on to the sleeve as shown in the picture. Paint a scary face with black Fabric paint.

BOTTLE CAP BONES

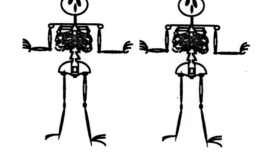

TO MAKE THIS CRAFT YOU NEED
White chenille stems
2 large white matching
plastic bottle caps
Black fabric paint
yellow garbage bag twist ties
Low melt glue gun
adult supervision

TO BEGIN

1. Glue the bottle caps to the top of a chenille stem.

2. Glue a garbage bag twist tie to the chenille stem to form the spinal column.

3. Bend garbage bag twist ties into an arc and glue to a chenille stem. Glue the arc from the spine to the front to form the rib cage. Repeat this procedure with two more chenille stems.

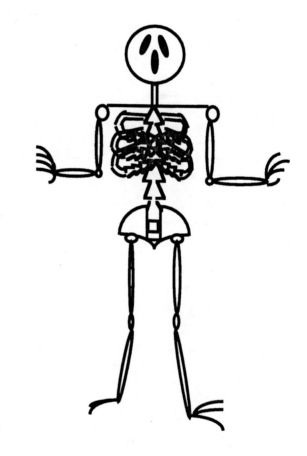

4. Glue small pieces of the chenille stem to the hand to form fingers.

5. Fold chenille stems in half at the waist to make hip bones and glue at the back of the spine.

6. Fold chenille stems in half at the and loop through the circles to make the leg bones bendable.

7. Glue small pieces of chenille stem to the foot to form the toes.

8. Use black fabric paint to paint a scary face on your bottle cap bones. Use him as a decoration or wear him to a party!

79

NOTES

NOVEMBER

POP TOP PILGRIMS

Pop Top Pilgrims hold napkins in place,
A bottle cap bottom, a bead for a face.
Arms made of Q-tips,
black felt makes their suit.
Adorning your holiday table so cute!

TO MAKE THIS CRAFT YOU NEED

2   dishwashing liquid push-pull tops
2   wooden painted bead faces
2   black chenille stems
4   Q-tips
1   square of black felt
1   square of white felt
Low melt Glue Gun
adult supervision

TO BEGIN

1. Pull the top portion off of the push-pull top from each cap. This craft requires only the bottom portion.

pop off top portion

2. Paint each cap with black fabric paint. Cover all the exposed surfaces and set aside to dry.

3. Cut each chenille stem in half and glue to the center tube of each cap. Leave the back open with the stems pointing towards the back.

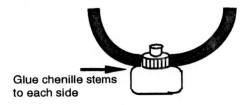

Glue chenille stems to each side

4. Cut two 1.5 inch squares of white felt. Cut a small slit in the center of each square. Bend the squares into a triangle and drape across the center tube covering the chenille stems.

5. Cut each Q-tip in half. Glue a small strip of black felt around each each tip to form the sleeves. Glue shut at the seams. Glue an arm on each side of the tube on each cap below the white collars.

Glue arms to each side of the center tube

Paint a black buckle in the center of the white band.

6. Glue a 16mm painted wooden bead face to the top of each tube above the white collar.

7. To form the lady pilgrim, glue a white felt square from the collar around the bead face to the opposite side. Cut a smaller square from black felt and glue it to the top of the white. Use Fabric paint to paint on a bow.
   LET DRY.

9. Tie napkins to the back of your pilgrims by twisting the chenille stems around them.

8. To make the hat for Mr.Pilgrim, cut a small black circle and a small black square from felt. Roll the square into a cone and glue it to the center of the circle to form the hat. Glue the hat to the top of his head. Paint a white strip band along the of the tube with fabric paint.
   LET DRY.

TWO LITER TURKEY

This 2-liter Turkey
wrapped in loopy chenille,
With popsicle legs, looks surprisingly real.
The talk of your Holiday table for sure.
Stuff him with napkins
or goodies galore!

TO MAKE THIS CRAFT YOU NEED
1 two liter plastic skirt shaped bottle
2 red plastic bottle caps
1 bag of brown loopy chenille
1 bag of red loopy chenille
2 popsicle sticks
2 dozen yellow plastic
garbage bag twist ties
White Fabric paint
Black Fabric Paint
Copper Fabric Paint
Low melt glue gun
adult supervision
Tacky glue

TO BEGIN
1. Cut the 2 liter bottle in half
    at the skirt indention. Use the
    bottom half of the bottle to
    collect your scraps of fabric.
    This craft requires only the
    top skirt shaped portion.

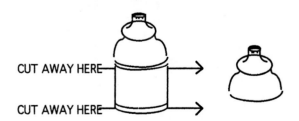

CUT AWAY HERE→

CUT AWAY HERE→

2. Glue your bottle caps together
    with Tacky glue and set aside to
    dry.

plastic bottle caps

    Glue Bottle caps together

3. Cut two 1/4 inch slit, below the
    rim of the bottle.

4. Starting at the base of the bottle,
    use the glue gun to glue loopy
    brown chenille around the
    entire bottle up to the rim.

5. Cut 3 plastic garbage twist ties
    to measure 1.5 inches long.
    Glue them together at the
    ends to shape the feet. Glue
    the claws to the bottom of
    popsicle sticks to create the
    legs.

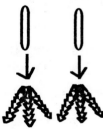

6. Glue red loopy chenille halfway around the dried bottle caps. Leave the excess hanging down. Glue a bent garbage bag twist tie on the seam side of the face for a beak.

7. Paint 8 garbage bag twist ties with copper fabric paint.

Let dry

Glue to the back end of the turkey for tail feathers.

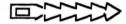

8. Paint 8 more twist ties with copper fabric paint.

Let Dry

Glue 4 on each side of the body for wings.

9. Paint the turkey face following the model shown or use your imagination and create your own

10. Stuff the opening at the back of the bird with decorative napkins and use him as the center piece for your holiday table.

LET US GIVE THANKS BY GIVING BACK TO THE WORLD

84

DECEMBER

A BOTTLE CAP
SNOWMAN DOLL

This Bottle Cap Snowman
is dressed in white felt,
You can keep him forever
because he won't melt!
His shiny top hat
fits his bottle cap head,
It keeps him warm
when he rides in a sled.
He loves to ice skate,
read books and to play,
A recycled doll
you'll be proud to display!

TO MAKE THIS CRAFT YOU NEED:
1 Two liter plastic bottle
2 white round plastic milk caps
1 square of white felt
1 square of black felt
Tacky Glue
Black Fabric Paint
Sparkle Varnish
Black chenille stems
Cotton balls

TO BEGIN:
1. Carefully cut the two liter
   bottle in half at the seam.
   Set aside. Glue the plastic caps
   together with tacky glue
   and let dry.

plastic bottle caps

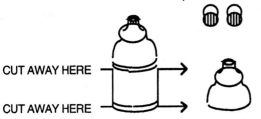

CUT AWAY HERE →

CUT AWAY HERE →

2. Cover the body in white felt
   and glue at the seam with a
   low melt glue gun.

COVER THE BODY IN WHITE FELT

3   Glue the dried bottle caps to
    the top of the body.

4.   Make a top hat out of black
     felt and glue it to the top of
     his head.

5. Cut two medium squares of white felt. Roll them into tubes and glue at the seams. Stuff each sleeve with cotton balls and glue to each side of the body for arms.

6. Use Sparkle Varnish to brush on snowy effects and shiny highlights on top of the white felt.

Let Dry

Use black fabric paint to paint a snowman face and buttons down the front. Bend chenille stems into a broom and glue in his hand with the glue gun.

TWIST TIE SNOWFLAKE

TO MAKE THIS CRAFT YOU NEED
8 yellow garbage bag twist ties
Tacky Glue
Crystal glitter
1 white chenille stem

TO BEGIN
1. Lay 8 twist ties on top of each
   otherto form a star.

2. Secure in the center with Tacky
   Glue and let set until dry.

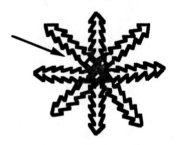

3. Once the snowflake is dry and stays
   in place when you lift it, brush the
   top with Tacky Glue and sprinkle
   crystal glitter on top of it to make
   it shine.   Let Dry.

glitter

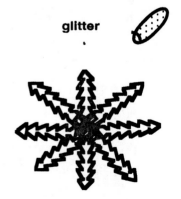

4. Repeat the same procedure
   on the opposite side and let
   dry.

5. Bend a chenille stem into a
   hook and knot it in the center
   of the snowflake through the
   hole opening.

6. Make a lot of them with
   different colored glitter to use
   for holiday decorations. You
   can also paint each twist tie in a
   different color

87

DISHWASHER DRUMMER BOY

The ribbons and wrappings,
and all of the trappings,
The holidays bring can astound you.
Look through different eyes,
and to your surprise,
Christmas is there all around you!
Plastic angel dolls, decorate all the halls,
fabric softner bells on the table,
A wreath made from caps, painted perhaps,
A laundry scoop cup for a stable.

TO MAKE THIS CRAFT YOU NEED:

1 dishwashing liquid push-pull top
        (Preferable the color blue)
1 painted wooden bead face
1 Q-tip
2 white plastic matching bottle caps
Tacky Glue
Low melt glue gun with adult supervision
Red Fabric paint
White Fabric paint
Blue fabric paint
1 small black pom-pom

TO BEGIN

1. Pull the top portion off of the push-pull top. This craft requires only the bottom portion.

pop off top portion

2. If the bottom portion is not the color blue, paint it blue with fabric paint and let dry before proceeding.

3 Glue the bottle caps together with Tacky glue and set aside to dry.

plastic bottle caps

 Glue Bottle caps together

4. Cut the Q-tip in half and glue it to each side of the center tube for arms. Paint the sleeves blue, leaving the Q-tip ends white.

Glue arms to each side of the center tube

5. Glue the painted bead face to the top of the center tube.

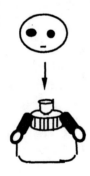

6. Glue the drummer boy to the top of the dried bottle caps in the center.

88

7. Paint red criss- crossing lines
   all around the caps. Let dry.

8. Dot the top of each criss-cross
   with white fabric paint. Let dry.

BOTTLE CAP CHRISTMAS TREE

TO MAKE THIS CRAFT YOU NEED
15 two liter plastic
matching bottle caps
Tacky glue
Q-tips
Glitter
(any color or a variety of colors)
Low melt glue gun
adult supervision
Variety of Christmas miniatures
or stickers
A bow to embellish

TO BEGIN:
1. Swirl a generous amount of
Tacky glue inside the hollow of
the 1st cap. Coat the bottom and
sides completely. Use a Q-tip
to ensure good coverage.

2. Fill the cap with holiday glitter
up to the rim. Turn the cap over
a folded piece of paper to catch the
excess. Tap the flat back of the cap
to recover any loose glitter.
Set aside to dry.

3. Repeat this procedure with the
remaining 14 caps.

4. Once dry, glue 5 bottle caps side
by side with the glittered hollows
facing forward.

5. On the second row, glue 4
bottle caps side by side on
top of the 1st row . Repeat
this procedure by gluing 3,
then 2, then 1 on top.

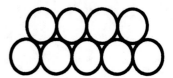

6. Spread tacky glue all around
the perimeter of the tree
outline.

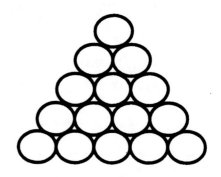

7. Starting at the bottom corner,
press green yarn into the glue.
Hold in place a few seconds
until set.

8. Rotate the yarn around the
perimeter of the tree
outline for two rows. When you
reach the center of the top cap,
STOP

90

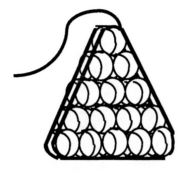

9. Make a six inch loop with the yarn and tie a simple slip knot at the base of the loop. Pull tightly on the yarn to shrink and center the knot.

HAPPY HOLIDAYS

10. Continue wrapping the yarn around the tree until all exposed areas are covered. Cut the yarn at the bottom of the tree and secure in place with glue.

11. To embellish your tree, glue miniatures, family pictures or stickers into the hollows. Glue a star or bow at the top of the tree to cover the knot. To further embellish your tree glue a beaded strand of pearls around the diameter.

ANGEL TREE TOPPER

With wings that are made from pleated white lace,
A 2-liter bottom, a bottle cap face,
This angel tree topper is unique in her trade,
Because she's recycled, handcrafted, homemade.
A flowing white gown and a red choir book,
A shiny gold bow and a heavenly look.
Now glue a small picture from someone you love,
And create a real angel sent down from above!

TO MAKE THIS CRAFT YOU NEED

1 plastic 2 liter skirt shaped bottle
2 white plastic matching bottle caps
1 yard of white lace
1 gold bow
Brown loopy
Small scrap of red felt
Black fabric paint
Low melt glue gun
adult supervision

TO BEGIN

1. Cut the 2 liter bottle in half
at the skirt indention. Use the
bottom half of the bottle
to collect your scraps of fabric.
This craft requires only the top
skirt shaped portion.

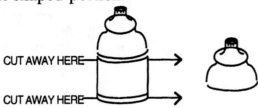

2. Glue your bottle caps
together with Tacky glue and
set aside to dry.

plastic bottle caps

   Glue Bottle caps together

3. Cut a 12 x 5 square of
white lace from your fabric.
Gather the lace at the edge
and glue directly to the rim
of the bottle.

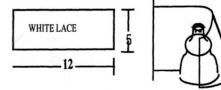

4. Glue the dried caps to the
top of the bottle.

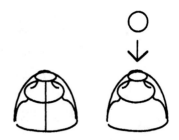

5. Cut two 3 x 5 inch squares
of lace from the fabric. Fold
the squares into cones and
glue along the seams to
secure.

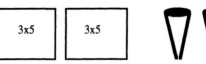

6. Glue the pointed end of each cone directly to the lace gown on the bottle on opposite sides of the body. Bend the arms at the elbow and glue directly to the fabric. Glue a gold bow or ribbon to the front of the lace gown.

9. Paint a singing exspression following the model shown or use your imagination and draw your own. Fold a small square of red ribbon or felt in half. Glue to the ends of the arms for a choir book.

7. Glue loopy brown chenille around the bottlecap head in the length you desire for the hair.

8. Cut two 4 x 4 squares of white lace. Fold each into tiny pleats and secure with the glue gun at the tip. Glue each wing to the back of the bottle on opposite sides.

BOTTLE CAP BELL

TO MAKE THIS CRAFT YOU NEED

1 bell shaped bottle cap
     (Shampoo, mouthwash, fabric
     softener)
Glitter (Any Christmas Color)
Tacky Glue
Q-tip
Holly sprigs or minature embellishments
1 jingle bell
Metallic bead cord (gold or silver)
Low melt glue gun
adult supervision

TO BEGIN

1. Drill a small hole through the top
     of the cap at the center.

2. Cut 6 inches of metallic bead cord
     from the skien. String the jingle
     bell through the cord and tie a knot
     at the open end. Use the glue gun to
     secure the knot. Pull the jingle bell
     down on top of the knot and hold it
     there a few seconds until set.

3. Push the cord from the bottom of
     the cap up through the hole in the
     center. Pull the cord up through the
     hole until the jingle bell reaches the
     top and will go no further.

4. Make a loop and tie simple
     slip knot at the base. Pull
     tightly on the cord, to
     shrink and center the knot.

5. Paint the body of the bell
     with Tacky Glue using a
     Q-tip. Use a thick coat for
     good coverage.

6. Sprinkle holiday glitter on
     top of the glue over wax
     paper to catch the excess.
     Let dry.

7. To embellish your bell,
     glue holly sprigs or
     Christmas miniatures at
     the top.

TWO LITER SANTA DOLL

With a musical touch tone glued at the rim,
A holiday Santa is perfect to trim.
Glue the red felt to the 2-liter base,
Red rosy cheeks and a bottle cap face!
A cotton ball beard and a black buckle belt,
A jolly exspression, a hat made from felt.
Make someone happy with this Santa doll,
Who'll bring Christmas tidings,
To one and to all!

TO MAKE THIS CRAFT YOU NEED

1   plastic 2-liter plastic
    skirt shaped bottle
2   white plastic matching bottle caps.
1   yard of red felt
1   square of black felt
1   bag of cotton balls
Tacky Glue
Two small white pom-poms
One musical Christmas touch tone.
Low melt glue gun
adult supervision
Black Fabric Paint

TO BEGIN

1. Cut the 2 liter bottle in half
    at the skirt indention. Use the
    bottom half of the bottle to
    collect your scraps of fabric.
    This craft requires only the
    top skirt shaped portion.

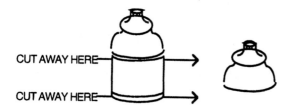

2. Glue your bottle caps
    together with Tacky glue
    and set aside to dry.

plastic bottle caps

 Glue Bottle caps together

3. Cut a red felt square that
    measures 12 x 5.   Start at
    the bottom of the bottle and
    glue the felt all around.
    When you reach the
    opposite side of the bottle,
    overlap the felt and glue in
    place with the glue gun.

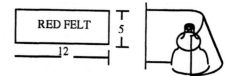

4. Turn the bottle so that the
    seam side is to the back.
    Make two pleats in the felt at
    the front. Glue directly to
    the bottle at two inches apart
    at the rim.

5. Cut a strip of black felt
    around the middle of
    the bottle below the pleats and
    glue in place at the back of
    the bottle overlapping at the
    fold. This creates Santa's
    belt.

95

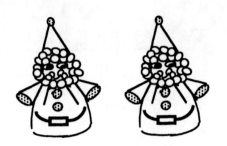

8. Glue the dried caps to the top of the bottle for the head.

7. Cut three red felt squares that measure 3x5. Fold into cones and glue at the seams. Glue a cotton ball at the wide opening of each cone. This creates two arms and a hat. Set aside.

8. Glue cotton balls around the head for hair and along the front for a beard.

9. Glue small white pom poms to the front of the chest for buttons.

10. Glue an arm on each side of the bottle underneath the beard.

11. Glue the last cone to the top of head for the hat.

12. Paint Santa's face with dimensional paint by following the model shown or use your own wonderful imagination and create your own.

Turn the bottle over and use the glue gun to glue a musical touch tone press inside the rim opening at the top of the bottle.

RECYCLE AND REUSE ALL YOUR CHRISTMAS WRAPPINGS!

CANDY CANE COTTAGE

TO MAKE THIS CRAFT YOU NEED

2 matching plastic laundry scoops
3 popsicle sticks
1 box of Q-tips
4 plastic candy canes
1 empty cereal box
28 plastic 2-liter break away rings
Red Fabric paint
Crystal Glitter
Tacky Glue
White felt
Low melt glue gun
adult supervision

TO BEGIN

1. Paint red stripes on the popsicles sticks with the red fabric paint and set aside to dry.

2. Open the cereal box at the seams and copy the dimensions from the diagram shown.

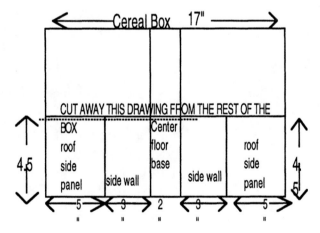

3. Glue white felt to one side of each roof panel the sidewalls and center floor base.

4. Use the glue gun to glue the laundry scoops back to back.

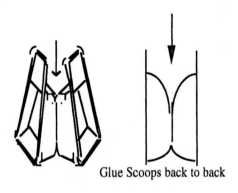

Glue Scoops back to back

5. Glue the 2 scoops along the center floor base of the cereal box. Fold the sidewall section up each side of the scoop and glue in place to secure. Be sure that the felt is on the outside.

6. Glue each roof panel to the top of the scoops. Glue at the sidewalls on each side to secure.

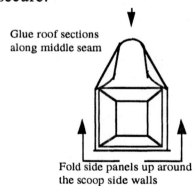

Glue roof sections along middle seam

Fold side panels up around the scoop side walls

7. Glue 1 painted popsicle stick along the center seam of the roof panels.

Glue a painted popscle stick along the top of the roof seams

8. Glue a painted popsicle stick along the front scoop openings on each side.

Glue a painted popsicle stick along the front scoop opening on each side of the cottage →

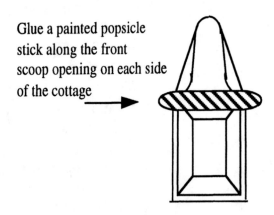

9. Glue 2-liter rings all along the roof and side panels.

Glue 2-liter break away rings all over the roof and side panels on both sides. →

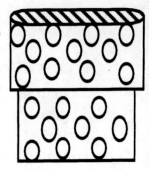

10. Glue plastic candy canes on each side of the front and back openings.

11. Pull the tips off of 2 dozen Q-tips. Glue all along the roof panel on both sides of the cottage.

Glue the tips of Q-tips hanging down the front to form icicles →

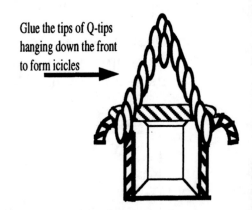

12. Dab Tacky glue in various places all over the cottage and sprinkle with crystal glitter for a snow covered effect.

13. Embellish the cottage by
    gluing holiday stickers or
    miniatures inside each plastic
    ring. Fill the openings with
    Christmas candy.

99

NOTES

CHAPTER 3

The

Bottle

Cap

BARNYARD

CRAFTS

BOTTLE CAP BEE

To make this cheerful bottle cap bee,
    Cut a plastic bottle in two,
Cover the body with yellow felt,
    Secure chenille stems
        with some glue.
Cut out some cereal wax paper wings,
    Glue in the middle behind,
To make his head use white bottle caps,
    Any round plastic you find.
Make anntenaes from 2 chenille sticks,
    Glue in the back of his face,
Now paint an exspression with fabric paint,
    You can follow a pattern or trace!
You'll just love this bottle cap bee,
    Created with your gentle touch,
It represents the care we share,
    for the planet we love so much!

TO MAKE THIS CRAFT YOU NEED
Tacky Glue
Black fabric paint
Black chenille stems
Cereal box was paper
Yellow felt
2 matching white plastic bottle caps
1 two liter plastic bottle
1 sheet of cereal box wax paper

TO BEGIN

1. Carefully cut the two liter bottle in half at the seam. Set aside.

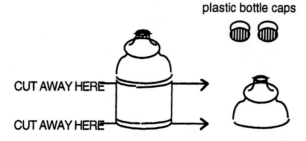

2. Glue the two bottle caps together with Tacky Glue and set aside to dry.

3. Wrap yellow felt around the top half of the bottle and secure in place with the glue gun.

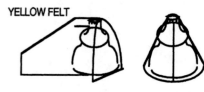

4. Glue bottle caps to the top of the bottle on top of the felt.

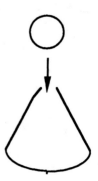

5. Wrap black chenille stems around the body and secure at the back with the glue gun.

6. Cut out wax paper wings and paint them lightly with tacky glue. Sprinkle crystal glitter on top of the glue to make them sparkle!

7. Glue the wings to the body of the bee at the back. Cut two small pieces of black chenille stems for antennae. Glue to the back of the bottle cap head.

8. Paint an expression on the face of your bee with black fabric paint. You can follow the patterns in the examples shown or use your imagination to create your own.

bottle cap bees!

BOTTLE CAP COW

How do you make a bottle cap cow?
What is the first thing you do?
Find a plastic 2-liter bottle,
And carefully cut it into!
Cover the body with soft white felt,
Now turn the base on its side.
Cover the opening left at the back,
(The part of the body that's wide)!
Now cover 4 small caps with felt,
To make his bottle cap toes.
Glue to bottom to balance his step,
Attach the tail where it goes.
Now trace a face from a square of brown felt,
Cut a circle to fit a round top.
Now glue the head to the neck of the bottle,
Right where it reaches a stop.
Embellish the body with spots of brown felt,
That's really all that you do.
You'll swear you'll hear the bottle cap cow,
Yell out a bottle cap, "Moo"!

TO MAKE THIS CRAFT YOU NEED
Tacky Glue
Black Fabric paint
1 square of white felt
1 square of brown felt
4 small plastic bottle caps
1 large white plastic bottle cap
1 two liter plastic bottle
Wiggle eyes

TO BEGIN
1. Carefully cut the two liter bottle in half at the seam. Set aside.

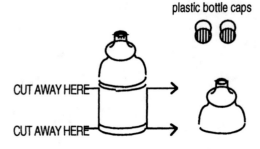

plastic bottle caps

CUT AWAY HERE

CUT AWAY HERE

2. Cover the body and the 4 small caps with white felt.

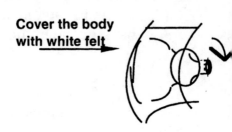

Cover the body with **white felt**

3. Cut out various shapes from brown felt and glue to the body.

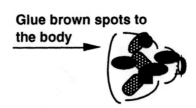

Glue brown spots to the body

4. Glue the legs to the bottom of the body.

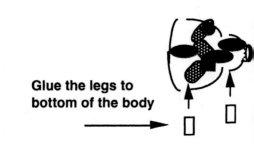

Glue the legs to bottom of the body

5. Cut out a cow face from a
   square of brown felt leaving
   an opening for round white
   bottle cap. Glue the felt
   around the cap.

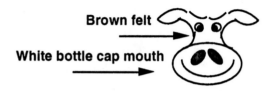

6. Glue wiggle eyes to the felt
   and secure the head to the body
   with a low melt glue gun.

moo

7. Cover the back open end with
   white felt and glue in place.
   Cut a small tail from brown
   felt and glue in the center.
   To further embellish, hang a
   small bell around the cow's neck.

BOTTLE CAP CHICK

Out in the barnyard, waiting for seed,
Is a bottle cap chick, waiting to feed.
A soft yellow body, a small orange beak,
With wiggle eyes open just for a peek!
Popsicle stick legs and twist tie toes,
Help him to walk wherever he goes!
Make one to share or make one to play,
He's waiting for you! Get started today.

TO MAKE THIS CRAFT YOU NEED
Tacky Glue
Yellow and Orange Fabric Paint
1 Square of yellow felt
1 Scrap of orange felt
1 Set of wiggle eyes
2 popsicle sticks
2 round plastic bottle caps
1 two liter plastic bottle
6 yellow garbage bag twist ties
Low melt glue gun

TO BEGIN
1. Carefully cut the two liter bottle
   in half at the seam. Set aside.
   Glue the plastic caps together with
   tacky glue and let dry.

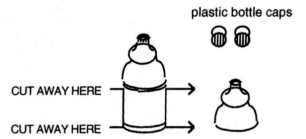

plastic bottle caps

CUT AWAY HERE →

CUT AWAY HERE →

2. Carefully cut two small holes
   just below the opening of the
   bottle wide enough for the
   popsicle sticks.

3. Turn the body on its
   side and cover it with
   yellow felt. Make small
   pencil marks for the
   two leg openings.

   Leave the excess felt to
   overhang at the back
   opening.

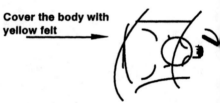

Cover the body with
yellow felt

4. Insert the popsicle sticks
   at the leg openings.
   Glue yellow plastic
   garbage bag twist ties to
   the legs and to form
   the toes. You can paint
   them with orange fabric
   paint.
   LET DRY

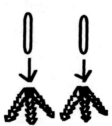

5. Gather the excess felt into a point and glue at the seam to form a tail. Use the glue gun to secure the dried bottle caps to the top of the body for the head. If you do not have yellow plastic caps to work with, just paint the caps you have, with yellow fabric paint. Push wiggle eyes into the wet paint on each side of the head.

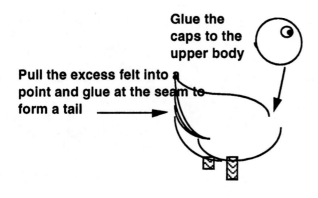

Glue the caps to the upper body

Pull the excess felt into a point and glue at the seam to form a tail ⟶

6. Glue and orange felt beak to your chick and he's ready to play!

TWO LITER TURTLE

Turtles live for years and years,
Close to the ground in a shell.
Wrinkled up skin,
hold secrets within,
To answers they will never tell.
Because they are wise,
Just look in their eyes.
They teach us in life to go slow.
By pacing our walk,
And thoughts when we talk,
We'll enjoy the world that we know!

TO MAKE THIS CRAFT YOU NEED
1 Two liter bottle
2 Green plastic bottle caps
Green Fabric paint
Black Fabric paint
1 square of green felt
1 large wooden spool
4 small wooden spools
Tacky glue
Wiggle eyes

TO BEGIN

1. Carefully cut the bottom dish from a two liter plastic bottle. Glue the bottle caps together with Tacky Glue and set aside.

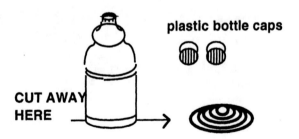

plastic bottle caps

CUT AWAY HERE

2. Cover the plastic bottom with green felt and secure in place with a low melt glue gun.

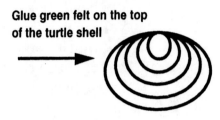

Glue green felt on the top of the turtle shell

3. Decorate the turtle shell by drawing different shapes on the felt with black fabric paint.

LET DRY

Decorate the shell with patterns and shapes

4. Glue a large wooden spool to the edge of the shell for the neck.

Glue an empty thread spool covered in green felt to the shell to make the neck.

5. Glue the dried caps to the top
    of the spool for the head.
    If you don't have green
    caps, use green fabric paint to
    paint them. Glue wiggle eyes to
    each side of the caps.
    Paint a smile with black
    fabric paint.

**Glue the dried caps to the top
of the spool to form the head.**

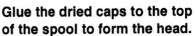

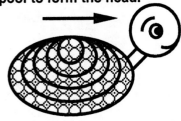

6. Glue 4 small wooden spools to
    the bottom of the shell for legs.
    Keep an eye on your turtle
    because turtles love to hide!

**Glue small
wooden spools
to the bottom for
legs.**

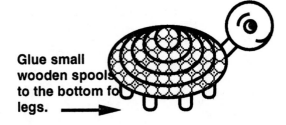

LADY BUG BOTTLES

RED FELT

Lady bug bottles
love to wear red,
With polka dot dresses
and wings
That they spread.
Fat pudgy cheeks
make leaves easy to munch,
Wouldn't you love
to invite one for lunch?

3. Glue the dried bottle caps to
    the top of the body to form
    the face. If you don't have
    black bottle caps, paint the
    caps with black fabric
    paint.
    LET DRY

TO MAKE THIS CRAFT YOU NEED
Tacky Glue
Black and White Fabric Paint
Wiggle eyes
Black chenille stems
1 square of red felt
1 Two liter plastic bottle
2 Round plastic bottle caps

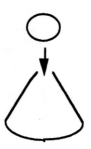

TO BEGIN
1. Carefully cut the two liter bottle
    in half at the seam. Set aside.
    Glue the plastic caps together
    with tacky glue and let dry .

4. Use black fabric paint to
    deocorate your lady bug
    with polka dots.
    LET DRY

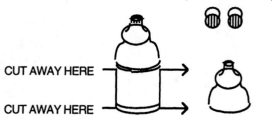
plastic bottle caps

CUT AWAY HERE
CUT AWAY HERE

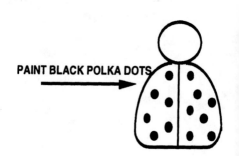
PAINT BLACK POLKA DOTS

2. Cover the body with red felt
    and secure at the seam with a
    low melt glue gun.

110

5. Glue two chenille stems to
    the back of the head for an
    antennae.

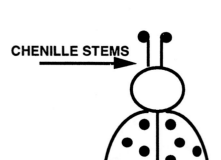

6. Glue wiggle eyes to the face
    and paint a smile with white
    fabric paint.

**Lady bug, Lady bug,
Don't fly away!
Teach us recycling is fun,
everyday!**

BOTTLE CAP OWL

Bottle cap owls
are wordly and wise
They see the planet
through their plastic eyes
They give a hoot for
recycling kids,
who craft and create
from throw away lids!!

TO MAKE THIS CRAFT YOU NEED
Tacky Glue
2 round plastic milk or o.j. caps
2 brown plastic animal eyes
50 plastic yellow garbage bag twist ties
1 two liter plastic bottle
brown, white and black fabric paint

TO BEGIN
1. Carefully cut the two liter bottle
    in half at the seam. Set aside.
    Glue the plastic caps together
    with tacky glue and let dry.

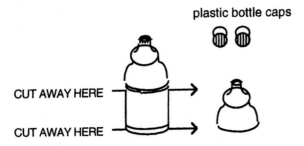

plastic bottle caps

CUT AWAY HERE

CUT AWAY HERE

2. Use the low melt glue gun to
    overlap twist ties pointing in
    the same direction around
    the body of the bottle.

Glue twist ties to the bottle
pointing in the same direction

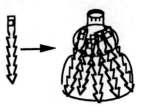

3. Glue the dried bottle caps to
    the top of the bottle.

Glue dried caps
to the top of the bottle

4. Start at the back of the
    bottle caps and over lap
    twist ties into a point at the
    front of the face. Secure in
    place with a low melt glue
    gun. Glue plastic animal
    eyes to the face. Paint a
    pointed nose with black
    fabric paint.
    LET DRY

Glue twist ties from the back of the caps to th
front in a point. Glue on wiggle animal eyes a
paint a pointed nose with fabric paint

5.   Glue the head to the body.

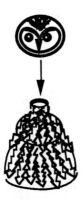

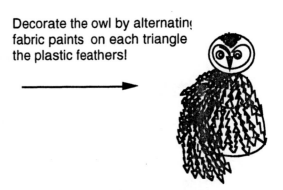

Decorate the owl by alternating
fabric paints on each triangle
the plastic feathers!

6.   Overlap additional twist ties
      on one side of the body to form
      a wing.

Overlap additional
twist ties along one
side of the body to
form a wing

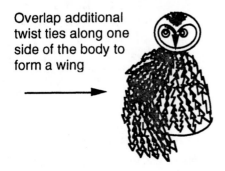

whoooooooooooooooo's
recycling?

7.   Embellish the owl further by
      paint each twist tie triangle a
      different color with fabric paint.

POP TOP PLASTIC PIGS

Plastic pigs never wear wigs!
They have the best manners at dinner.
Use them as banks or decorative dolls,
And be a recycling winner!

TO MAKE THIS CRAFT YOU NEED
1 two liter plastic bottle
2 round plastic milk or O.J. caps
1 square of pink felt
Black Fabric paint
Wiggle eyes
4 plastic calculator or
register paper rolls
 or (4 small plastic 2 liter bottle caps)
Tacky Glue
Low melt glue gun

TO BEGIN
1. Carefully cut the two liter bottle
     in half at the seam. Set aside.
     Glue the plastic caps together with
     tacky glue and let dry.

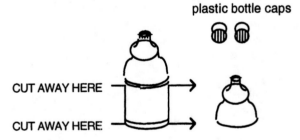

plastic bottle caps

CUT AWAY HERE

CUT AWAY HERE

2.   Cover the top half of the bottle
      with pink felt and secure in
      place with glue gun.

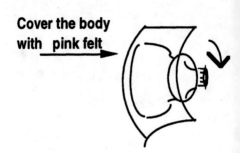

Cover the body
with pink felt

3. Cover the small dish at the
     bottom of the bottle with
     pink felt. Secure it in place
     with a glue gun. Glue the
     uncovered side to the pig's
     body to cover the opening.

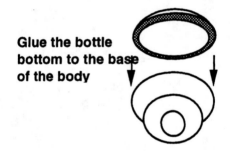

Glue the bottle
bottom to the base
of the body

4.   Cover the dried bottle caps
      with pink felt. Cut small
      triangles from felt for
      ears and glue to the caps.
      Glue wiggle eyes to the
      face and paint a nose,
      cheeks and smile with
      black fabric paint.
      LET DRY

Glue the dried face to neck opening
of the bottle with a low melt glue gun.

5. Cover four calculator or register
rolls with pink felt.
(You can substitute small
plastic bottle caps for the paper
rolls. Secure in place with glue.
Glue the covered rolls to the
bottom of the pig body at an
angle, to balance.

**Glue legs in
place at an
angle**

6. Glue a twisted pink chenille
stem to the back for a tail.
To make your pig a bank, cut
an opening in the top middle
of the back.

115

FARMER JOHN

Farmer John, stands stall with his hoe,
 He runs the recycling farm,
With bottle cap chicks and pigs in a pen,
And roosters that sound the alarm.
With two liter turkeys and bottle cap bugs,
And a bottle cap barn down the way,
Farmer John lives a pleasant life,
 Conserving his caps everyday!

TO MAKE THIS CRAFT YOU NEED

Tacky Glue
Black fabric paint
1 two liter plastic bottle
2 round white plastic bottle caps
1 square of plaid material
1 square of blue-jean material
4 black chenille stems
1 small doll straw hat

TO BEGIN

1. Carefully cut the two liter bottle in half at the seam. Set aside. Glue the plastic caps together with tacky glue and let dry.

CUT AWAY HERE →

2. Glue your bottle caps together with Tacky glue and set aside to dry.

3. Cut the plaid material in half and glue to the top half of the bottle.

(ADULT SUPERVISION REQUIRED)

4. Cut the left over plaid material in half and roll each half into a tube. Glue along the seam with a low melt glue gun.

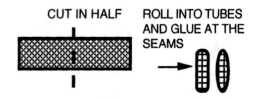

CUT IN HALF

ROLL INTO TUBES AND GLUE AT THE SEAMS →

5. Glue the arms to the back of the bottle extending outward.

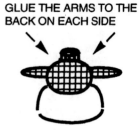

GLUE THE ARMS TO THE BACK ON EACH SIDE

116

6. Wrap blue jean material around the bottom half of the bottle. Secure in place around the base of the bottle with a low melt glue gun.

WRAP BLUE JEAN AROUND THE WAIST AND GLUE AT THE BACK SEAM

7. Glue chenille stems over the shoulders for suspenders and around the waist for a belt. Glue dried caps to the top for a head.

Farmer John

GLUE DRIED CAPS TO THE TOP

8. Paint a face on Farmer John with black fabric paint. Bend chenille stems to form a hoe and secure in place with glue. To complete Farmer John glue a small straw hat to the top of his head.

117

COUNTRY KELLIE DOLL

Country Kellie fills her basket with flowers,
She loves the outdoors and the trees.
She uses her head to bake bottle cap bread,
With honey from bottle cap bees.
Her dress is from scraps, with a bonnet perhaps,
She makes a great friend, when you play.
It doesn't take much, just your special touch,
So make Country Kellie, today!

TO MAKE THIS CRAFT YOU NEED
Tacky Glue
Black Fabric Paint
1 two liter plastic bottle
2 white plastic bottle caps
1/2 yard country print fabric
1 small ribbon (any color)
Low melt glue gun
Two cotton balls

TO BEGIN
1. Carefully cut the two liter bottle in half at the seam. Set aside. Glue the plastic caps together with tacky glue and let dry.

CUT AWAY HERE

2. Glue your bottle caps together with Tacky glue and set aside to dry.

3. Cut the country print material in half. Use enough of one piece to glue around the top portion of the bottle.

(ADULT SUPERVISION REQUIRED)

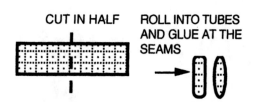

4. Cut two small squares from the left over scrap and roll each into tubes. Glue at the seams with a low melt glue gun.

CUT IN HALF   ROLL INTO TUBES AND GLUE AT THE SEAMS

5. Glue the arms to the back of the bottle. Wrap two cotton balls in the print fabric and secure at the top of each should with a low melt glue gun.
GLUE THE ARMS TO THE BACK ON EACH SIDE

6 . Starting at the back of the bottle, glue the large piece of material to the waist. Pleat the material as you go and secure each pleat with the glue gun. This creates a full skirt.

PLEAT EACH PIECE AS YOU GO

7. Glue the dried caps to the top of the bottle for the head. Glue Glue a large print circle to the back of the cap for a bonnet.

Glue a small straw basket with minature flowers in her hand.

BOTTLE CAP BARN

The Bottle Cap Barn,
Has laundry scoop stalls.
A cereal box, cut in half,
Makes the walls!
Red felt is glued to the sides,
Roof and floor,
Popsicle sticks make the fence,
And the door!
Stuff it with popouri or with hay,
A cute country craft,
The recycling way!

TO MAKE THIS CRAFT YOU NEED
1 empty cereal box folded flat
2 laundry plastic laundry scoops
2 squares of red felt
1 chenille stem
1 plastic push-pull top
4 plastic yellow garbage bag ties
Rust colored fabric paint
Low melt glue gun
Popouri or straw

TO BEGIN

1. Cut the cereal box in half across the middle.

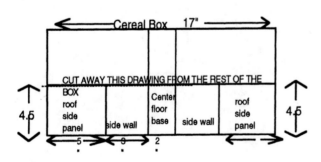

2. Cut the roof side base from the side wa

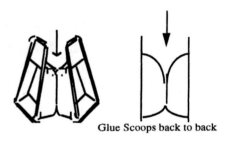

3. Using the glue gun, glue the laundry scoops back to back.

Glue Scoops back to back

4. Place them in the middle of the center b floor base. Fold up the side panels and secure to the scoops

Glue roof sections along middle seam

5. Glue popsicle sticks in a row along the top of the roof.

Glue popsicle sticks along
the roof panels

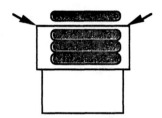

6. Bend a chenille stem into a hook. Push the straight end of the stem through a push-pull top and secure in place with glue.

Bend a chenille stem into a small
hook and push the straight end
through the push pull top.

7. Glue four yellow twist ties into a cross.

Glue four yellow ties into a cross.
leave the hole in the middle open.

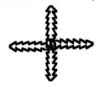

8. Set the cross on the hook of the chenille.
DO NOT GLUE TO THE STEM!
Allow the windmill to spin.

Set twist ties on the hook of the chenille.
DO NOT GLUE. This windmill needs to spin.

9. Glue the windmill to the top of the barn.

Glue the windmill to the top of the barn

10. Glue popsicle sticks at the front of one side of the barn for a door. Paint the popsicle sticks with rust fabric paint.
LET DRY

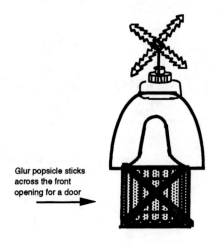

Glur popsicle sticks
across the front
opening for a door

11. Stuff the inside hollows of the
roof with popouri or straw!

NOTES

NOTES

CHAPTER 4

THE

BOTTLE

CAP

GAMES

BOTTLE CAP
CHECKER BOARD GAME

TO MAKE THIS CRAFT YOU NEED

1 cereal box open and folded flat
1 ruler
Red paint
Black paint
24 plastic bottle caps (the same size)
1 black marker

TO BEGIN

1. Make the checker board by drawing 64 equal squares on the open cardboard cereal box. Use the ruler to measure squares exactly. Use the marker to draw the squares.

CEREAL BOX FOLDED FLAT. USE A BLACK MARKER TO DRAW THE SQUARES.

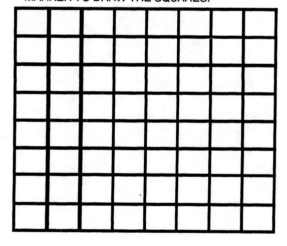

2. Paint every other square black and every other square red. (Let Dry)

3. Paint the tops of 12 bottle caps red and more black. (Let Dry)

4. Now play to win!

MULTIPLICATION
BOTTLE CAPS

TO MAKE THIS GAME YOU NEED :
  81 PLASTIC BOTTLE CAPS
9 ROWS OF 9 SAME COLORED CAPS:
  FOR EXAMPLE:

9 GREEN	9 BLUE	9 WHITE
9 ORANGE	9 RED	9 YELLOW
9 PURPLE	9 BROWN	9 PINK

(If you don't have the right colors for
your caps, just paint the flat top with
fabric paint and let dry)

You also need 81 white circles cut from a
poster board the exact diameter of each
cap.
  Use a cap to trace.
Tacky glue
1 black marker
1 empty shoebox

TO BEGIN

1. Seperate the caps into 9 rows
   each of the same color. Follow
   the pattern shown to make the
   game. Use a different color cap
   for each times table.

2. Write the solutions to the top half
   of the cap on a white circle and
   use tacky glue to secure the circle
   in place.

3. Once all the caps have dried toss
   all the caps into the shoe box.
   Each child reaches in the box and
   pulls out a problem.

   If he or she gets the answer
   right, she gets to keep the
   cap and keep going. Once an
   answer is guessed wrong, the cap
   is returned to the box and moves
   on the the next player.

4. The player with the most colored
   caps at the end of the games
   wins!!!!!!!!

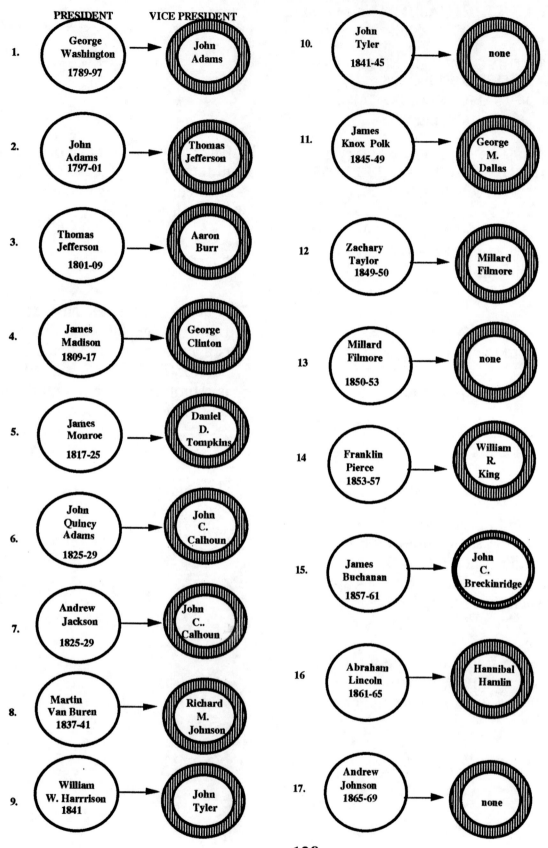

PRESIDENT   VICE PRESIDENT

1. George Washington 1789-97 → John Adams

2. John Adams 1797-01 → Thomas Jefferson

3. Thomas Jefferson 1801-09 → Aaron Burr

4. James Madison 1809-17 → George Clinton

5. James Monroe 1817-25 → Daniel D. Tompkins

6. John Quincy Adams 1825-29 → John C. Calhoun

7. Andrew Jackson 1825-29 → John C. Calhoun

8. Martin Van Buren 1837-41 → Richard M. Johnson

9. William W. Harrrison 1841 → John Tyler

10. John Tyler 1841-45 → none

11. James Knox Polk 1845-49 → George M. Dallas

12. Zachary Taylor 1849-50 → Millard Filmore

13. Millard Filmore 1850-53 → none

14. Franklin Pierce 1853-57 → William R. King

15. James Buchanan 1857-61 → John C. Breckinridge

16. Abraham Lincoln 1861-65 → Hannibal Hamlin

17. Andrew Johnson 1865-69 → none

128

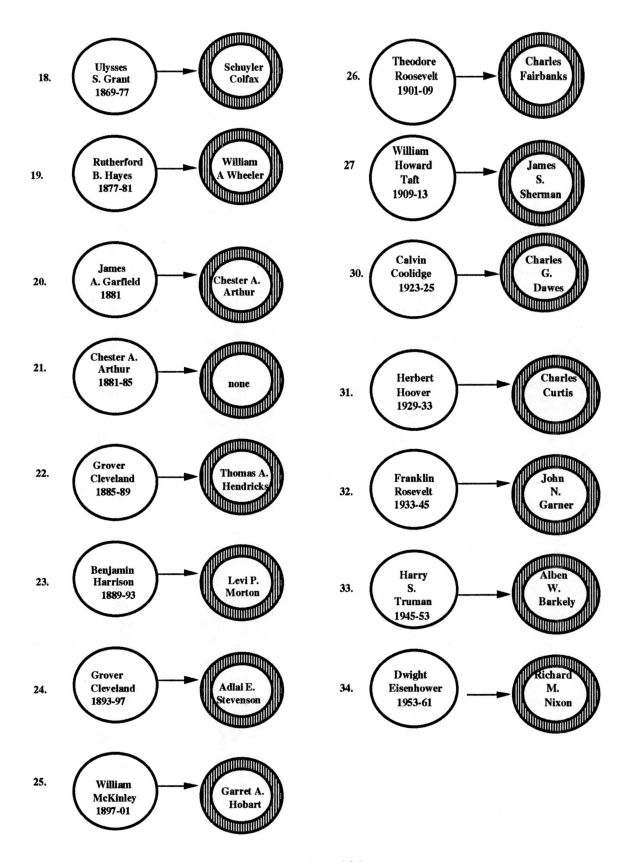

18. Ulysses S. Grant 1869-77 → Schuyler Colfax

19. Rutherford B. Hayes 1877-81 → William A Wheeler

20. James A. Garfield 1881 → Chester A. Arthur

21. Chester A. Arthur 1881-85 → none

22. Grover Cleveland 1885-89 → Thomas A. Hendricks

23. Benjamin Harrison 1889-93 → Levi P. Morton

24. Grover Cleveland 1893-97 → Adlai E. Stevenson

25. William McKinley 1897-01 → Garret A. Hobart

26. Theodore Roosevelt 1901-09 → Charles Fairbanks

27 William Howard Taft 1909-13 → James S. Sherman

30. Calvin Coolidge 1923-25 → Charles G. Dawes

31. Herbert Hoover 1929-33 → Charles Curtis

32. Franklin Rosevelt 1933-45 → John N. Garner

33. Harry S. Truman 1945-53 → Alben W. Barkely

34. Dwight Eisenhower 1953-61 → Richard M. Nixon

129

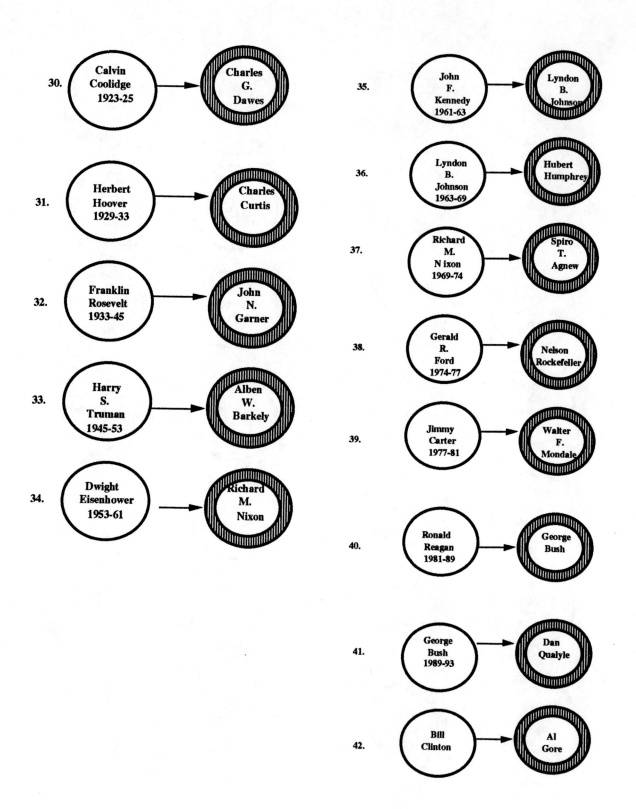

30. Calvin Coolidge 1923-25 → Charles G. Dawes

31. Herbert Hoover 1929-33 → Charles Curtis

32. Franklin Rosevelt 1933-45 → John N. Garner

33. Harry S. Truman 1945-53 → Alben W. Barkely

34. Dwight Eisenhower 1953-61 → Richard M. Nixon

35. John F. Kennedy 1961-63 → Lyndon B. Johnson

36. Lyndon B. Johnson 1963-69 → Hubert Humphrey

37. Richard M. Nixon 1969-74 → Spiro T. Agnew

38. Gerald R. Ford 1974-77 → Nelson Rockefeller

39. Jimmy Carter 1977-81 → Walter F. Mondale

40. Ronald Reagan 1981-89 → George Bush

41. George Bush 1989-93 → Dan Qualyle

42. Bill Clinton → Al Gore

BOTTLE CAP
CLASSROOM CAPITALS

TO PLAY THIS GAME YOU NEED

51 plastic bottle caps (any color)
51 round white circles
     cut from white paper
     (the same diameter
     of the bottle cap)
Black fabric paint or a black marker
A list of all the states
and their capital cities
Tacky glue
1 shoe box

TO BEGIN

1. Use the marker or paint to
   label the flat side of each bottle
   cap with a state abbreviation.
   If using (paint) let dry
   before proceeding.

2. On the white circles label
   the capital city of each state.
   Use the Tacky Glue to secure the
   proper city with the appropriate
   state.

3. Once listed and glued toss all the
   caps into a large empty shoe box.

4. To play the game, each child
   reaches into box and pulls out a cap.
   If he pulls out the cap with the
   abbreviations facing up, he must
   name the state it represents. If he
   pulls up the side with the capital
   city, he must name the state it
   belongs to. If he gets it right,
   he keeps the cap at his desk and
   continues. If he misses the box goes
   on to the next   player.

The player that has the most caps
when the box is empty
WINS!!!!!!!!!!!!!

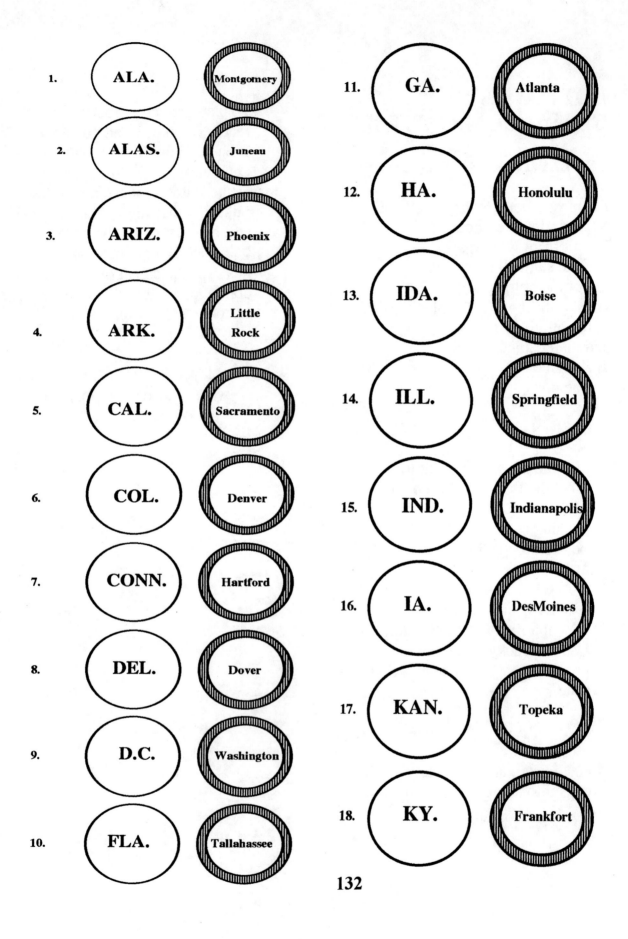

1. ALA. — Montgomery
2. ALAS. — Juneau
3. ARIZ. — Phoenix
4. ARK. — Little Rock
5. CAL. — Sacramento
6. COL. — Denver
7. CONN. — Hartford
8. DEL. — Dover
9. D.C. — Washington
10. FLA. — Tallahassee
11. GA. — Atlanta
12. HA. — Honolulu
13. IDA. — Boise
14. ILL. — Springfield
15. IND. — Indianapolis
16. IA. — DesMoines
17. KAN. — Topeka
18. KY. — Frankfort

132

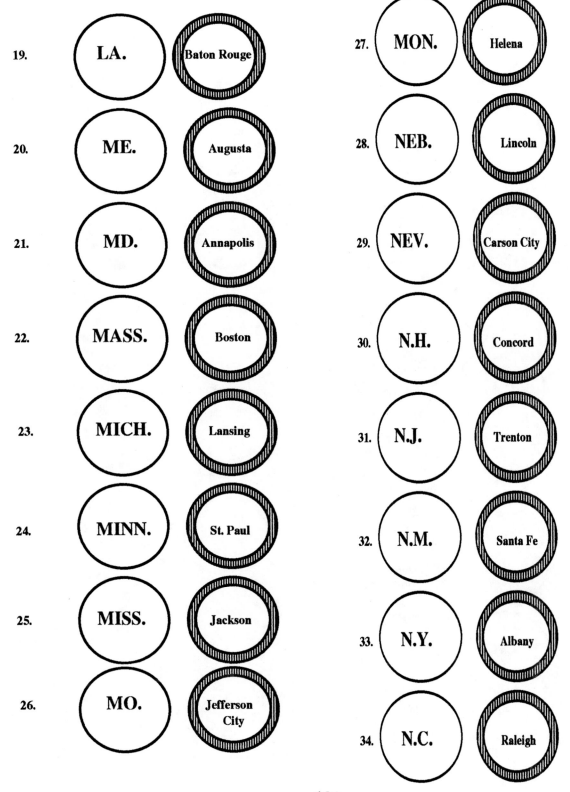

19. LA. — Baton Rouge

20. ME. — Augusta

21. MD. — Annapolis

22. MASS. — Boston

23. MICH. — Lansing

24. MINN. — St. Paul

25. MISS. — Jackson

26. MO. — Jefferson City

27. MON. — Helena

28. NEB. — Lincoln

29. NEV. — Carson City

30. N.H. — Concord

31. N.J. — Trenton

32. N.M. — Santa Fe

33. N.Y. — Albany

34. N.C. — Raleigh

133

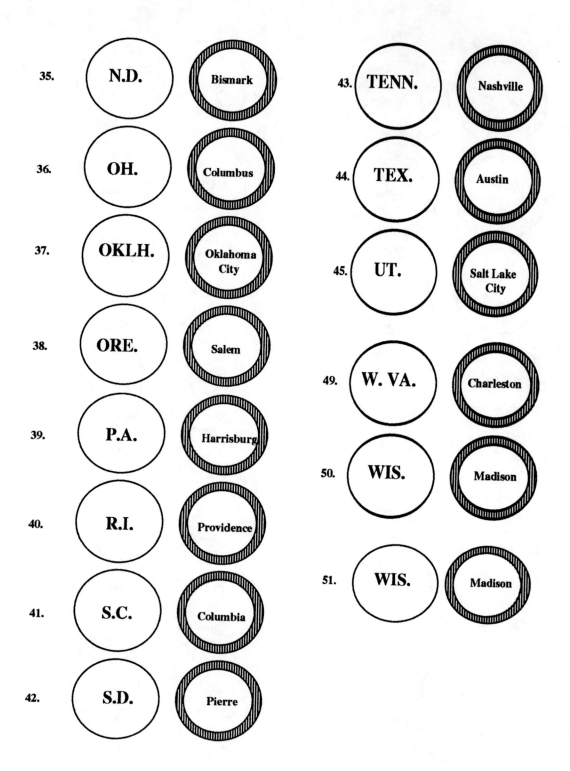

35. N.D. — Bismark

36. OH. — Columbus

37. OKLH. — Oklahoma City

38. ORE. — Salem

39. P.A. — Harrisburg

40. R.I. — Providence

41. S.C. — Columbia

42. S.D. — Pierre

43. TENN. — Nashville

44. TEX. — Austin

45. UT. — Salt Lake City

49. W. VA. — Charleston

50. WIS. — Madison

51. WIS. — Madison

BOTTLE CAP
CLASSROOM CATERPILLAR

TO MAKE THIS CRAFT YOU NEED

1 plastic bottle cap per student
3 or 4 squares of white felt
tacky glue
1 chenille stem
Black Fabric paint
scissors
Low melt glue gun (Adult supervision)

1. Cut each photograph the size of the inside diameter of each cap.

PHOTOGRAPH

cut photograph

bottle cap
inside
diameter

2. Place tacky glue inside the diameter of the cap and push the photograph inside the cap and on top of the glue.

3. Cut a small strip of white felt the same diamter as the width of the cap. Use the glue gun to secure the felt to the edge of each cap.

Glue each cap to the next

5. Leave one cap at the begining of the caterpillar and use fabric paint to make a face.   Let dry.

glue chenille stems at the top of the head!

135

BOTTLE CAP CONCENTRATION
CAPS
TO PLAY THIS GAME YOU NEED:

24 plastic bottle caps the same size.
Stickers, paint, markers , pictures or
photographs.

TO BEGIN:

1. Design pairs of bottle that match
    by using pictures cut from
    magazines, photographs, or by
    painting symbols on the flat top of
    the caps.   Make 12 matching sets
    and let dry.

2. Mix up the pictures and place
    them face down on a table.
    Each player takes turns trying to
    guess where the matching sets are.
    The player with the most matches
    wins!!!!

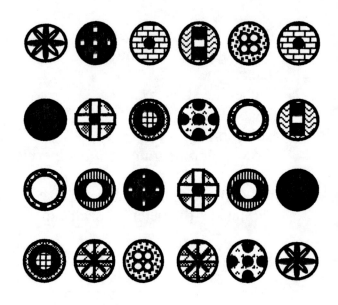

Find the matches!

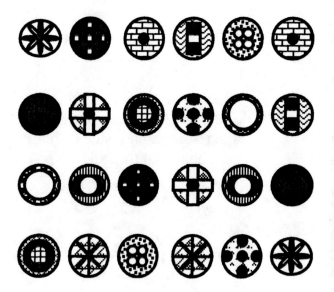

136

TIC TAC TOE TOPS

TO MAKE THIS GAME YOU NEED

9 Plastic bottle caps and color
Black fabric paint or a black marker
I empty cereal box folded flat
8 black chenille stems

TO BEGIN

1. Open the cereal box and lay it flat.
    Glue the chenille stems to the
    cereal box following the patterns
    shown.

2. Use markers or fabric paint
    to paint on and X and and O
    on the caps of your choice.
    Let Dry

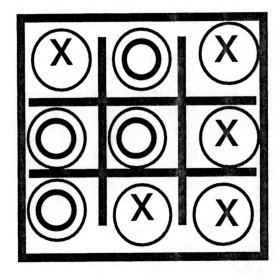

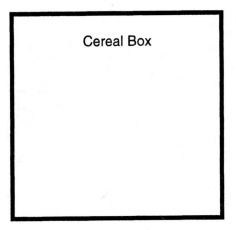

Cereal Box

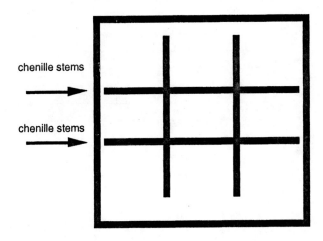

chenille stems

chenille stems

137

NOTES

CHAPTER 5

The

Bottle

Cap

COSTUMES

&

POSTERS

CAST OF CHARACTERS AND POSTER DIAGRAMS

Children should be grouped into twelve month categories. Each team month works together on their theme posters, character costumes and songs or poems. The entire class works on rehearsing ensemble songs throughout the play. Suggested student numbers for team months may vary according to the number of students.

JANUARY TEAM

This group consists of four main characters.

1. **Betty Bottlecap**
   A girl who wears a white poster board costume and ponytails in her hair.

2. **Billy Joe Bottlecap**
   A boy who wears a white posterboard costume and a backward baseball cap.

3. **2-Liter Bottle**
   A boy or girl who carries a long white bottle shaped poster.

4. **Narrator**
   A boy or girl who reads the script at a podium.

JANUARY BOTTLE CAP COSTUMES

1. Betty Bottle Cap and Billy Joe Costumes

Use a large posterboard to cut out a round circle.

Paint the inside diameter with light blue paint leaving a four inch frame around the blue circle.

Cut a matching circle for the back side of the costume but leave it white.

Glue four strips of felt 4 inches wide from one circle to the other so that the costume may be slipped over the head.

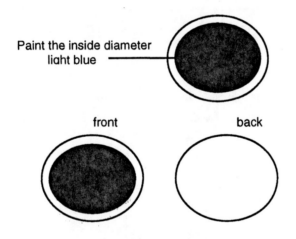

Paint the inside diameter
light blue

front   back

Glue felt strips from front to the back

The 2 Liter Bottle Costume

Cut out the shape of a bottle from two poster boards glued together to give it length. Decorate the top of the bottle by painting lines to form a cap. The bottle can be held at the center indentation.

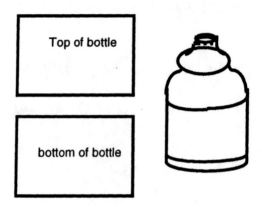

Paint lines at the top of the bottle to form cap

POSTER DESIGN

Use a low melt glue gun to glue
bottle caps to the poster board

142

FEBRUARY COSTUMES

This group consists of five main characters.
Three front girls and two back up girls all dressed in red.
Girls should wear long pop top pendants they can twirl as they sing.

FEBRUARY FLAPPER GIRLS AND BOW TIE BOYS

Girls should dress in pink or red dresses to the knee. They should wear bottle cap headbands, pop-top pendants, bottle cap bracelets and dishwasher dinner rings.

Boys should wear white long sleeve shirts, dress slacks and bottle cap bow ties.

glue a bottle cap in the center for *bow tie*

POSTER DESIGN:

MARCH TEAM

This group consist of three main characters.
In the center is a boy Leprechaun.
He wears a round hat a yellow vest and a red fuzzy beard.
Two girls stand dressed in green on each side of the Leprechaun and sing the
song 2-Liter Larry.

LARRY LEPRECHAUN COSTUME

Make a white or yellow vest from felt to fit the person. Glue shamrocks make from
green caps directly to the vest. A green hat can also be decorated with shamrocks
the same way. Students behind Larry should dress all in green.

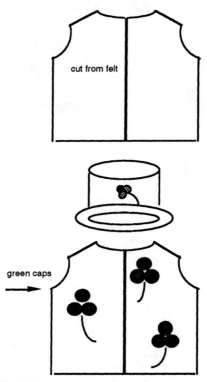

POSTER DESIGN

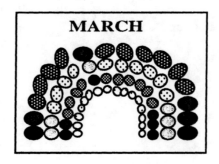

APRIL TEAM

This group consists of a variety of boys and girls who dress in bright pastel spring colors and flowery outfits. Bonnets and casual dress will meet the theme.
These children form a line across the stage to sing ,
"Before we let go of the   world we know".

APRIL COSTUMES

Students should wear all bottle cap rainows in different colored that are glued to tee shirts. Another option would be outlining the globe in a circle of caps.

rainbows of caps!!!

POSTER DESIGN

Glue green bottle caps to form an earth circle

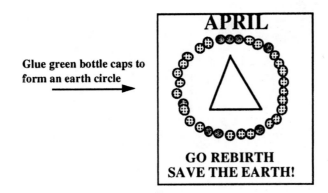

APRIL

GO REBIRTH
SAVE THE EARTH!

MAY TEAM

This group consist of a variety of boys and girls all dressed in soft blue.
They form a line across the stage to recite the poem
"POP TOP PICTURE FRAME".

MAY COSTUMES

Students can glue glittered caps in the shape of a frame to tee shirts or a light blue dress.

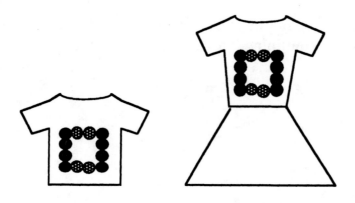

POSTER DESIGN

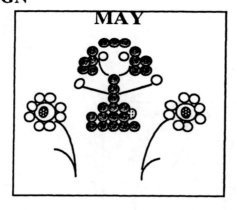

MAY

146

JUNE TEAM

This group consists of a variety of boys and girls who dress in purple attire.
Girls wear purple blouses, dresses or skirts and boys wear purple tee shirts
or purple bow ties against white dress shirts. These children line up   across the
stage to sing the song , "If We Look To The Sky".

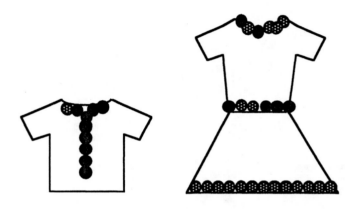

POSTER DESIGN:

JULY TEAM
This group consists of a
Bottle Cap, Clown, a Ring Master, Uncle Sam, and The Bottle Cap Band

Costumes should be designed with as many bottle caps as possible.
The Bottle Cap Band group consists of a band member who carries a tamborine
made of bottle caps, a band member with a keyboard made from bottlecaps,
a drummer who carries a bottle cap drum made from an old coffee can and bottle
cap drum sticks and a band member who carries Bottle cap clackers and jingle bell
bracelets.

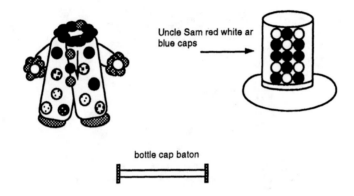

Uncle Sam red white ar
blue caps

bottle cap baton

POSTER DESIGN

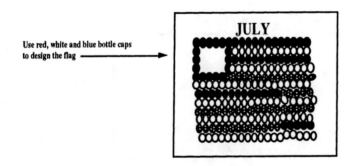

Use red, white and blue bottle caps
to design the flag

JULY

148

AUGUST TEAM

This group consist of a variety of children who wear glasses, carry backpacks and bookmarks,crayons and school props. Boys can wear suspenders and knee socks, girls can wear pony tails. These children line across the stage to recite the poem, "School Esstentials".

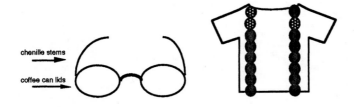

chenille stems

coffee can lids

POSTER DESIGN:

Back to school bookmarks made from yarn wrapped popsicle sticks and bottle cap tops.

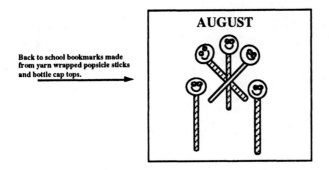

AUGUST

SEPTEMBER TEAM

This team consists of three boys dressed as Patches the Plastic Scarecrow . Boys should wear straw hats, white gloves and design a green felt coat with bottle cap buttons and orange felt patches.

Each boy should carry a broom on their shoulder as they recite the poem,
"PATCHES".

Three girls also appear in this group dressed in Indian atire. Each Girl should wear a poncho and headbands with garbage bage yellow twist tie feathers.

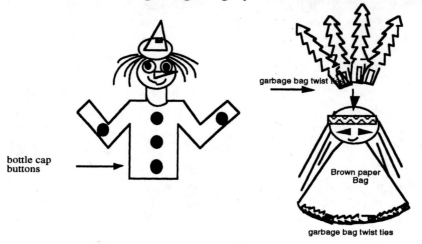

POSTER DESIGN

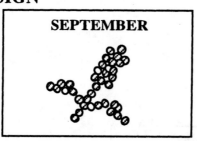

OCTOBER TEAM

This group consist of a bottlecap count Dracula, a bottlecap creature,
a plastic poltergeist, a witch who stands center stage, and various plastic
pumpkin people. They recite a Halloween poem.

POSTER DESIGN:

NOVEMBER TEAM

This group consists of a variety of boys and girls dressed in pilgrim and Indian costumes. They line up across the stage to sing , "A Sacred Loan".

POSTER DESIGN:
   A bottlecap cornacopia.

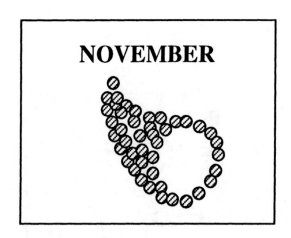

DECEMBER TEAM

This group consists of six angels, 1 drummer boy and a bottlecap Santa Claus
with a bottlecap beard. The children   unite across the stage to sing,
 "Christmas is there all around you".

DECEMBER COSTUMES

This group consists of Angels with garbage   bag twist tie wings glued to poster
boards. Also a Santa with a bottle cap beard.

BOTTLE CAPS GLUED TO
FELT
→

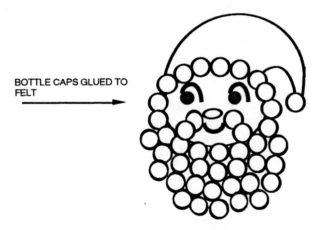

POSTER DESIGN:

DECEMBER

BOTTLE CAP BALLERINAS

Two girls dressed in pink leotards and tights can decorate a skirt with bottlecaps to be bottlecap ballerinas. These girls carry the posters across the stage in between acts to announce the upcoming month.

NOTES

NOTES

Chapter 6

THE

BOTTLE

CAP

MUSICAL

PLAY

THE BOTTLE CAP KIDS
Earth Day Musical Play

Written By: Kathy Cisneros
Music By: Lynn Darden

This inovative earth day musical incorporates various elements of education. It combines art and music, recycling and science into an exciting and informative production. To begin this project, children needs to begin collecting plastic bottle caps at the begining of the school year to complete the projects and posters they will need for their April Earth Day performance.

In science class, children should set aside time each week to clean and dry the bottle caps and then group them into colors for storage.

In art class, children should be grouped into teams representing the months of the year so that you have twelve groups of children.

Each team will make posters out of the bottle caps with a theme representing the month they represent.

All costumes should be decorated with bottle caps as well. In music class, the children can work on the group songs as well as theme songs for specific months. The combination of these diverse classes motivates the children into working toward an Earth Day Celebration!

BOTTLE CAP KIDS

Written By : Kathy Cisneros
Music By: Lynn Darden

STAGE DIRECTION
The children divide on stage into two groups facing each other
(Side A and Side B).
Side A begins by leaning forward and asking the questions.
Side B leans forward when they respond.
Both sides will rock back and forth during the introduction.

Side A:
EVERYBODY'S TALKING BOUT RECYCLING.

Side B: **(LET'S HEAR IT!)**

Side A:
TURNING ALL THE GARBAGE INTO CASH.

Side B: **(YOU KNOW IT!)**

Side A:
SAVING ALL THE ARTICLES THEY ASK FOR.

Side B: **(WITH SPIRIT)**

Side A:
CONDENSING ALL THE ITEMS IN THE TRASH.

Side B: **(DON'T THROW IT!)**

Side A:
BUT NOW WE NEED TO KNOW ABOUT THE PLASTIC.

Side B: **(THE BOTTLES?**

Side A:
NO, NOT THE BOTTLES BUT THE LIDS.

Side B: (WHAT'S UP NOW?)

Side A:
THEY'RE FILLING UP THE LANDFILLS
ON THE PLANET.

Side B: (YOU'RE KIDDING?)

Side A:
IT'S TIME TO EMPOWER ALL THE KIDS.

Side B: (WITH ACTION!)

STAGE DIRECTION
Both sides turn and face the audience.

Side A:
WE'LL FORM A BOTTLE CAP COALITION!

Side B: (GET READY!)

Side A:
SAVING ALL THE PLASTIC CAPS WE FIND.

Side B: (YOU GOT IT!)

Side A:
IN EVERY HOME IN THE CITY.

Side B: (LET'S DO IT!)

Side A:
WE'LL START BY RECYCLING THE MIND!

Side B: (YOU KNOW IT!)

Side A:
WE'LL MAKE PROJECTS FROM THE
BOTTLE CAPS COLLECTED!

Side B: (THE COLORS!)

Side A:
EACH MONTH WE'LL CREATE
A BRAND NEW THEME.

Side B: (FOR SEASONS!)

Side A:
AND WE'LL TEACH WHAT WE LEARN
TO OUR PARENTS.

Side B: (LET'S SHOW EM!)

Side A:
INTRODUCE THEM TO THE BOTTLE CAPPING DREAM!

Side B: (GET STARTED!)

STAGE DIRECTION

The children immediately begin to sing "Go Rebirth, Save the Earth". During this
song, the four January characters leave the stage to slip on their costumes.

GO REBIRTH SAVE THE EARTH LYRICS AND SHEET MUSIC

All:
SEE THE WORLD THROUGH DIFFERENT EYES,
FIND A BETTER WAY!
RECYCLE THINGS FROM HOME SUPPLIES,
YOU USE EVERY DAY!

CHORUS:
GO REBIRTH! SAVE THE EARTH!
SIMPLIFY YOUR PLAN.
GO REBIRTH! SAVE THE EARTH!
EVERYBODY CAN!

ALL:
DON'T BUY MORE THAN WHAT YOU NEED,
IT ENDS UP IN THE TRASH!
YOU WASTE IT ALL BECAUSE OF GREED,
WHILE BLOWING ALL YOUR CASH.

CHORUS:
GO REBIRTH! SAVE THE EARTH!
SIMPLIFY YOUR PLAN.
GO REBIRTH! SAVE THE EARTH!
EVERYBODY CAN!

ALL:
SHARE YOUR IDEAS AND CREATE, FOR PURPOSE AND FOR FUN,
GIFTS AND TOYS FOR GIRLS AND BOYS, AND THAT HELPS EVERYONE!

CHORUS:
GO REBIRTH! SAVE THE EARTH!
SIMPLIFY YOUR PLAN.
GO REBIRTH! SAVE THE EARTH!
EVERYBODY CAN!

ALL:
IF EVERYBODY DID THEIR PART, THE WORLD WOULD WIN THE RACE.
THERE IS NO TIME TO PUT IT OFF,
WE'RE RUNNING OUT OF SPACE!

CHORUS:
GO REBIRTH! SAVE THE EARTH!
SIMPLIFY YOUR PLAN.
GO REBIRTH! SAVE THE EARTH!
EVERYBODY CAN!

"GO REBIRTH SAVE THE EARTH" - 1st Song

STAGE DIRECTION:
All students shout in unison:

All:
GO REBIRTH! SAVE THE EARTH!
SIMPLIFY YOUR PLAN.
GO REBIRTH! SAVE THE EARTH!
EVERYBODY CAN!

STAGE DIRECTION:

At the end of this song, two bottle cap ballerinas carry the "HAPPY NEW YEAR" poster made out of bottlecaps across the stage. The four January characters come out in costume through the middle from behind the the students who remain on stage. One student is dressed as a 2-liter plastic bottle, he stands at stage left. He is followed by Billy Joe bottlecap and Betty bottlecap. Another student stands at stage right with a script. This student is the narrator who tells the story the children act out. The two bottle caps stand in a line taking tiny baby steps toward the 2-liter bottle as the narrator reads.

JANUARY

NARRATOR:
Betty was a bouncing baby bottle cap. When she was born, she was diapered with a plastic blue liner. She was perfectly round and symmetrical in shape.

Betty followed all the other baby bottle caps down an electric assembly line to a 2-liter transport bottle.

When her turn came, Betty jumped on her transport and twisted around to lock her seatbelt in place. Then she began a long journey. Betty's transport bottle was loaded with many others into a jam packed crate. The crate was then loaded on to a long moving chamber. She looked around in the darkness and saw hundreds of baby bottle caps! Suddenly, the chamber hit a bump in the road and Betty banged her head into the head of a boy bottle cap.

STAGE DIRECTION:

Betty softly bumps Billy Joe

Betty: "Sorry." said Betty.

Billy: "It's okay."

Narrator: said the boy cap.

Billy: "What's your name?"

Betty: "Betty. What's yours?"

Billy: "Billy-Joe. Billy Joe bottle cap."

Betty: "What a cool name! Billy do you know where we are going?"

Billy: "Sure, every cap kid knows that!"

Betty: "Well, I don't and I'm scared. Won't you please tell me, Billy?"

Narrator: **she asked batting her bottle cap baby blue eyes at him.**

Billy: "To the Marketplace."

Betty: "Marketplace? Where is that?"

Billy: "That's where all the brand new bottle caps go until they're selected.

Betty: "Selected for what."

Narrator: she asked nervously.

Billy: "For a purpose. Don't you know anything?"

Betty: "What's a purpose? And why do YOU know so much about it anyway?"

Narrator: Billy-Joe shook his head.

Billy: "Girls."

Narrator: he whispered.

Billy: "I heard the big caps talking, you know, the milk and the orange juice caps. They were huddled in a group when I was being diapered and I heard them!"

Betty: "What else did they say, Billy?"

Billy: "Well, it seems when you're selected, you're taken to a huge place filled with people until you've served your purpose.

Betty: "What do you mean?"

Billy: "I really don't understand it myself, but pray you don't get selected right away."

Betty: "Why not?

Billy: "Because if you're selected right away, then it won't be long before you've served your purpose and then it's over."

Narrator: Betty twisted completely around.

Betty: "Over? What do you mean over? Do we go back to the Marketplace, the transports, the assembly line?"

Billy: "From the way I hear it, only the transports are taken back to the assembly line."

Narrator: said Billy.

Billy: "They are recycled."

Narrator: Betty's transport bottle began to smile.

Betty: "What happens to us? Where do we go?"

Billy:
"Most of the time, we're just thrown away!"

Narrator: answered Billy.

Betty: "Thrown away?"

Billy: "Yeah, one of the big caps was saying there's a plastic bottle cap graveyard filled with millions of us!"

Betty: "But that doesn't serve any purpose! There has to be a better way. We shouldn't be made to live for such a short period of time and then just thrown away!"

Billy:	"Yeah, well there's nothing you can do about it!"
Narrator:	Said Billy.

Betty:	"Maybe not you! But I'm not staying here!"
Narrator:	said Betty. She mustered all her strength and began twisting off of her transport.
Billy:	"What are you doing?"
Narrator:	Cried Billy-Joe.
Betty:	"I'm going to find that graveyard and round up my relatives!"
Billy:	"What for?"
Narrator:	asked Billy.
Betty:	"To form a bottle cap coalition. Together, we'll find a way to serve another purpose!"
Billy:	"You're crazy!"
Narrator:	yelled Billy.
Betty:	"Well, from the way I see it, I really don't have much to lose."
Narrator:	said Betty turning her last twist before breaking free. All the baby bottle caps began whispering in disbelief.

STAGE DIRECTION:
Students in the back begin whispering amongst themselves.

Narrator: No baby bottle cap had ever taken such a stand before.
Billy thought carefully about what Betty had said.
Life for a bottle cap didn't seem to hold much promise or
opportunity. He decided to join Betty on her quest to serve
an additional purpose. So Betty and Billy rolled off their
2-liter transports and passed all the other baby bottle caps.
When the moving chamber came to a complete stop and the
back door opened, the rebellious bottle caps rolled away.

STAGE DIRECTION:
ALL FOUR JANUARY STUDENTS
REPEAT THE NEXT FOUR LINES TOGETHER.

All Four:
Saving the planet begins with you!
The bottle caps show you what you can do.
Look twice at things before you throw.
Let's get started with the show!

STAGE DIRECTION:
As the four students leave the stage, the bottle cap ballerinas carry the Heart shaped
poster made out of bottle caps across the stage for February. As the poster is going
across, the Pop-top girls get into position on stage for the poem,
POP TOP PENDANTS.

FEBRUARY

Girl 1:
IF YOU WANT TO BE MY VALENTINE,
JEWELRY IS THE KEY.
A BOTTLE CAP COLLECTION
WOULD MEAN THE MOST TO ME.

CHORUS ALL GIRLS:
POP-TOP PENDANTS ON A STRING,
BOTTLE CAPS ALL THROUGH MY HAIR.
BRACELETS UP AND DOWN MY ARM,
WOULD SHOW HOW MUCH YOU CARE.
JUST DON'T BRING ME CANDY BARS,
OR OTHER CHOCOLATE THINGS.
JUST FILL ALL MY FINGERS WITH,
DISHWASHER DINNER RINGS!

Girl 2:
DRESS ME UP IN PLASTIC TOPS,
EMBELLISH THEM WITH PEARLS,
THEY'RE PERFECT GIFTS FOR VALENTINES,
ESPECIALLY FOR GIRLS!

CHORUS ALL GIRLS:
POP-TOP PENDANTS ON A STRING,
BOTTLE CAPS ALL THROUGH MY HAIR.
BRACELETS UP AND DOWN MY ARM,
WOULD SHOW HOW MUCH YOU CARE.
JUST DON'T BRING ME CANDY BARS,
OR OTHER CHOCOLATE THINGS.
JUST FILL ALL MY FINGERS WITH,
DISHWASHER DINNER RINGS!

Girl 3:
BY RECYCLING YOUR GIFT TO ME,
YOUR LOVE FOR ME WOULD SHINE.
SO POP YOUR TOP AND FLIP YOUR LID,
AND BE MY VALENTINE!

CHORUS ALL GIRLS:
POP-TOP PENDANTS ON A STRING,
BOTTLE CAPS ALL THROUGH MY HAIR.
BRACELETS UP AND DOWN MY ARM, WOULD SHOW HOW MUCH YOU CARE.
JUST DON'T BRING ME CANDY BARS,
OR OTHER CHOCOLATE THINGS.
JUST FILL ALL MY FINGERS WITH, DISHWASHER DINNER RINGS!

STAGE DIRECTION:
All students shout in unison:

All:
GO REBIRTH! SAVE THE EARTH!
SIMPLIFY YOUR PLAN.
GO REBIRTH! SAVE THE EARTH!
EVERYBODY CAN!

STAGE DIRECTION:
As the February girls leave the stage, the ballerinas carry the rainbow poster made out of plastic bottle caps across the stage. Behind them the Leprechaun stands in center stage as he entire class recites, 2-Liter Larry.

MARCH
ALL STUDENTS:

AT THE END OF A RAINBOW,
HIS STORY IS TOLD,
2-LITER LARRY WITH
POTS FULL OF GOLD.
A RED FUZZY BEARD,
A FULL JOLLY GRIN,
A ROUND PLASTIC BELLY
FOR COINS TO FIT IN.
EXTENDING HIS ARMS
TO GRANT EVERY WISH,
A BUCKLE DOWN VEST,
A ROUND PLASTIC DISH.
A BLACK BUCKLE HAT
THAT'S GREEN AT THE RIM,
A 2-LITER LEPRECHAUN,
LARRY THAT'S HIM!

STAGE DIRECTION: All students shout in unison:

All:
GO REBIRTH! SAVE THE EARTH!
SIMPLIFY YOUR PLAN.
GO REBIRTH! SAVE THE EARTH!
EVERYBODY CAN!

STAGE DIRECTION:
As the Leprechaun leaves the stage, the ballerinas carry the
"Go Rebirth! Save the Earth!" poster across the stage.
As they cross, a group of children get into position on stage to sing the song,
"Before we let go of the world we know."

BEFORE WE LET GO OF THE WORLD WE KNOW
LYRICS AND SHEET MUSIC

APRIL GROUP:

WE CAN'T SIT BY AND NOT EVEN TRY,
AND WATCH IT ALL SLIP AWAY.
WE MUST PACK AND PRESERVE,
FOR OUR CHILDREN DESERVE,
AN ENVIRONMENT WHERE THEY CAN PLAY.

WE SHOULDN'T WEAR MASKS,
TO COMPLETE ALL OUR TASKS,
FACE A CONCRETE WORLD WITHOUT SPACE,
BY CREATING THIS MESS,
WE'RE CAUSING DISTRESS, WITH GARBAGE ALL OVER THE PLACE!

STAGE DIRECTION:
ALL STUDENTS ON STAGE SING THE CHORUS AS THEY SWAY BACK AND
FORTH TO THE BEAT.

CHORUS:
SO BEFORE WE LET GO OF THE WORLD THAT WE KNOW,
LEAVING SOLUTIONS BEHIND US,
WE LOOK TO THE TREES THAT BATHE IN THE BREEZE,
KNOWING THEY'RE HERE TO REMIND US.

THAT NOTHING IS WORTH, POLLUTING THIS EARTH,
AND LEAVING THE PLANET IN SORROW.
BY CHANGING OUR WAYS WE'LL ENSURE OUR DAYS,
FROM TOMORROW'S CHILDREN WE BORROW.

IF WE WANT TO PREVAIL, WE MUST FIRST BLAZE A TRAIL.
BY DOING THE THINGS WE ARE PREACHING.

BY GIVING RESPECT, WE CONSERVE AND PROTECT
THE WORLD FULL OF CHILDREN WE'RE TEACHING.

CHORUS:

SO BEFORE WE LET GO OF THE WORLD WE KNOW,
LEAVING SOLUTIONS BEHIND US,
WE LOOK TO THE TREES THAT BATHE IN THE BREEZE,
KNOWING THEY'RE HERE TO REMIND US.
THAT NOTHING IS WORTH, POLLUTING THIS EARTH,
AND LEAVING THE PLANET IN SORROW.
BY CHANGING OUR WAYS WE'LL ENSURE OUR DAYS,
FROM TOMORROW'S CHILDREN WE BORROW.

IT JUST TAKE A SEED TO GROW WHAT YOU NEED,
IN A GARDEN YOU'VE PLANTED FROM REASON.
THAT SUPPLIES EVERYONE WITH KNOWLEDGE AND FUN,
THAT CONTINUES FROM SEASON TO SEASON.

CHORUS:
SO BEFORE WE LET GO OF THE WORLD WE KNOW,
LEAVING SOLUTIONS BEHIND US,
WE LOOK TO THE TREES THAT BATHE IN THE BREEZE,
KNOWING THEY'RE HERE TO REMIND US.
THAT NOTHING IS WORTH, POLLUTING THIS EARTH,
AND LEAVING THE PLANET IN SORROW.
BY CHANGING OUR WAYS WE'LL ENSURE OUR DAYS,
FROM TOMORROW'S CHILDREN WE BORROW.

STAGE DIRECTION:
All students shout in unison:

All:
GO REBIRTH! SAVE THE EARTH!
SIMPLIFY YOUR PLAN.
GO REBIRTH! SAVE THE EARTH!
EVERYBODY CAN!

"BEFORE WE LET GO OF THE WORLD WE KNOW" - 2nd Song, April

MAY GROUP:

BY GLUING FOUR CAPS
IN A ROW, AT THE TOP.
FOUR ON EACH SIDE,
THE BOTTOM, THEN STOP.
BALANCE EACH SIDE
TO MEASURE THE SAME,
THE RIGHT COMBINATION
FOR MAKING A FRAME.
FILL EVERY HOLLOW WITH
GLITTER AND GLUE,
EMBELLISH WITH ROSES,
A BOUQUET OR TWO.
INSERT YOUR BEST PICTURE,
OR DRAWING OR POEM,
AND GIVE AS A GIFT,
TO BE HUNG IN YOUR HOME!

All:
GO REBIRTH! SAVE THE EARTH!
SIMPLIFY YOUR PLAN.
GO REBIRTH! SAVE THE EARTH!
EVERYBODY CAN!

JUNE

STAGE DIRECTION:

As the May group exit the stage, the ballerinas carry a bottle cap bow tie poster for Father's Day across the stage. As they cross, the June group get into position to sing their song, "If we look to the sky".

IF WE LOOK TO THE SKY LYRICS AND SHEET MUSIC

JUNE GROUP:

SO MANY THINGS TO REMEMBER, SO MANY RULES TO OBEY,
SOME THINGS YOU HAVE TO RECYCLE, OTHERS YOU JUST THROW AWAY.
YOU HAVE TO LOOK FOR THE NUMBERS,THEY TELL YOU WHAT YOU CAN THROW,
BUT I JUST LOOK OUT MY WINDOW, FOR SECRETS THE ANIMALS KNOW.

CHORUS:

IF WE LOOK TO THE SKY, AND THE BIRDS THAT FLY HIGH,
WE'LL SEE THEIR RESPECT FOR THE PLANET.
THEY TAKE WHAT THEY NEED, FOR SHELTER AND FEED,
WITHOUT TAKING ONE THING FOR GRANTED.
WATCHING THE CARE , THEY HAVE IN THE AIR,
WE MUST LEARN FROM THESE CREATURES.
DEMONSTRATING THEIR GRACE, WHILE CONSERVING THEIR SPACE,
THEY ARE THE BEST OF OUR TEACHERS,

SOMETIMES THE BEST THINGS ARE BASIC, USING THE LEAST TO GET THROUGH.
JUST LIKE THE ANIMAL KINGDOM,
WE SHOULD FOLLOW THE THINGS THAT THEY DO.
THEY KNOW THAT EVERYTHING'S PRECIOUS,
EACH TWIG BUILDS A NEST THAT THEY SHARE.
EACH LEAF AND EACH STONE, IS A TREASURE ALONE,
FOR THE CREATURES, THAT TAKE TO THE AIR.

CHORUS:

IF WE LOOK TO THE SKY, AND THE BIRDS THAT FLY HIGH,
WE'LL SEE THEIR RESPECT FOR THE PLANET.
THEY TAKE WHAT THEY NEED, FOR SHELTER AND FEED,
WITHOUT TAKING ONE THING FOR GRANTED.
WATCHING THE CARE, THEY HAVE IN THE AIR,
WE MUST LEARN FROM THESE CREATURES.
DEMONSTRATING THEIR GRACE, WHILE CONSERVING THEIR SPACE,
THEY ARE THE BEST OF OUR TEACHERS.

(REPEAT AND FADE)
THEY ARE THE BEST OF OUR TEACHERS,

"IF WE LOOK TO THE SKY" - 3rd Song, June

179

STAGE DIRECTION:
All students shout in unison:

All:
GO REBIRTH! SAVE THE EARTH!
SIMPLIFY YOUR PLAN.
GO REBIRTH! SAVE THE EARTH!
EVERYBODY CAN!

STAGE DIRECTION:
AS JUNE EXITS THE STAGE, THE BALLERINAS CARRY THE
BOTTLE CAP FLAG POSTER ACROSS THE STAGE TO ANNOUNCE
JULY. AS THEY CROSS, A BOTTLE CAP CLOWN, A JUGGLER,
UNCLE SAM AND A RING MASTER POSITION THEMSELVES ON
STAGE TO SING.

IT'S THE 4TH OF JULY LYRICS AND SHEET MUSIC

JULY GROUP:
IT'S THE 4TH OF JULY! IT'S RED, WHITE AND BLUE.
A HOT AIR BALLOON, AND A YO-YO OR TWO,
WILL ENHANCE ANY PARTY, ERASE ANY FROWN.
CHEERS FROM THE CROWD, FOR THE BOTTLE CAP CLOWN!
NOW, HERE TODAY, TO SING AND TO PLAY.
IT'S THE BEST IN THE LAND,
IT'S THE BOTTLE CAP BAND!

STAGE DIRECTION:
ENTER A GROUP OF CHILDREN HOLDING BOTTLE CAP INSTRUMENTS.
FEATURED ARE A BOTTLE CAP KEYBOARD, BOTTLE CAP CASTANETS, A BOTTLE
CAP TAMBORINE AND A BOTTLE CAP DRUM.

WHOLE CAST:
HERE'S A KEYBOARD MADE OF CAPS! LOTS OF COLORS AND PERHAPS
JINGLE BELLS, JUST HEAR THEM PLAY, WE RECYCLE EVERYDAY!
WITH BOTTLE CAPS WE BEAT THE DRUM, TIE A STRING AND LET THEM HUM.
HEAR THE MUSIC IN THE AIR, WE RECYCLE EVERYWHERE!
THE CASTENETS ARE MADE FROM TOPS, THAT WE PULLED OFF ALL THE POPS.
AND THE BEST YOU'VE EVER SEEN, IS OUR CAPPING TAMBORINE!
HEAR THE MUSIC , SPREAD THE NEWS, RETURN TO BASICS AND REUSE,
BEFORE YOU THROW IT ALL AWAY, SAVE THE PLANET EVERYDAY!
WE'RE THE CAPPING COALITION, AND RECYCLING IS OUR MISSION.
WHEN WE START UNTIL WE'RE DONE, WE MAKE ALL ARE PROJECTS FUN!

"IT'S THE 4TH OF JULY" - 4th Song, July

181

STAGE DIRECTION:
All students shout in unison:
All:
GO REBIRTH! SAVE THE EARTH!
SIMPLIFY YOUR PLAN.
GO REBIRTH! SAVE THE EARTH!
EVERYBODY CAN!

STAGE DIRECTION:
AS THE JULY GROUP EXITS THE STAGE, THE BALLERINAS CARRY THE POSTER ACROSS FEATURING THE BOTTLECAP BOOKMARKS TO ANNOUNCE AUGUST WITH A BACK TO SCHOOL THEME. THE AUGUST GROUP STAND ON STAGE WITH BOOKS, BACKPACKS AND SCHOOL SUPPLIES AS THEY RECITE THEIR POEM.

AUGUST GROUP:

WE HAVE ALL OUR SCHOOL ESSENTIALS,
BACKPACKS, BOOKS AND SHARPENED PENCILS
PAPER, RULERS, SCISSORS, GLUE,
FOLDERS, MARKERS, CRAYONS TOO.
BUT THE BEST TOOLS WE CAN TAKE ,
ARE THE ONES WE LOVE TO MAKE.
WITH SOME YARN AND PLASTIC LIDS,
WE MADE BOOKMARKS FOR THE KIDS.
A POPSICLE STICK WAS USED AS BASE,
TO HOLD OUR FAVORITE STORY'S PLACE.
KEY CHAINS MADE FROM CAPS AND RINGS,
POGS AND STICKERS, TOYS AND THINGS.
BACK TO CLASSROOMS, TEACHERS, RULES,
USING BOTTLE CAPS AS TOOLS!
ENJOYING ALL THE THINGS YOU MADE,
"RECYCLING" YOU MAKE THE GRADE!

STAGE DIRECTION:
All students shout in unison:

All: GO REBIRTH! SAVE THE EARTH!
SIMPLIFY YOUR PLAN.
GO REBIRTH! SAVE THE EARTH!
EVERYBODY CAN!

STAGE DIRECTION:
AS THE AUGUST GROUP LEAVES THE STAGE, THE BALLERINAS CARRY A POSTER SHOWING A BOTTLE CAP CORN, REPRESENTING A FALL HARVEST. AS THEY CROSS THE STAGE, THREE SCARECROWS POSITION THEMSELVES ON STAGE FOR
THE SONG, "PATCHES AND PRINCESS".

PATCHES AND PRINCESS LYRICS AND SHEET MUSIC

SEPTEMBER GROUP:
SCARECROWS:

PATCHES WAS BORN
WITH A BOTTLE CAP HEAD.
COVERED IN PLASTIC
FROM A WARM LOAF OF BREAD.
DRESSED IN GREEN FELT
WITH A PATCH ON HIS COAT.
A CHENILLE STEM IS TWISTED
AROUND HIS WIDE THROAT.
HE'S WEARING WHITE GLOVES
FOR SCARING THE BIRDS.
HE DOES IT WITH SILENCE
WITHOUT ANY WORDS.
BUT PATCHES STANDS TALL,
HE'S ANXIOUS TO PLAY.
RECYCLE YOUR BOTTLES
AND DO IT TODAY!

STAGE DIRECTION:
AT THIS POINT, THREE INDIAN PRINCESS GIRLS JOIN THE SCARECROWS ON STAGE TO SING THE "INDIAN PRINCESS SONG"

ALL GIRLS SING:
LONG BLACK SHINY HAIR THAT FALLS TO HER FEET,
THIS INDIAN PRINCESS IS REALLY QUITE SWEET!
HER PAPER BAG PONCHO AND SLEEVES FROM THE PIECES
ARE SHAPED WHEN YOU FOLDAND YOU PRESS OUT THE CREASES.
NOW ZIG-ZAG- THE PAINT,AND TRIM UP THE BASE,
CAREFULLY PAINT A SWEET INDIAN FACE.
MAKE A PAPOOSE AND GLUE IN HER HANDS,
EMBELLISH THE COLLAR JUST THE FOLLOW THE BANDS!
HER GARBAGE BAG TWIST TIES MAKES FEATHERS FROM PLASTIC.
RECYCLE YOUR SCRAPS TO MAKE SOMETHING FANTASTIC!

"PATCHES AND PRINCESS" - 5th Song, September

OCTOBER

STAGE DIRECTION:
AS SEPTEMBER GROUP LEAVES THE STAGE, THE BALLERINAS CARRY THE
BOTTLE CAP "BOO" POSTER ACROSS THE STAGE REPRESENTING
HALLOWEEN. AS THEY CROSS, BOTTLE CAP COUNT DRACULA, A PLASTIC
POLTERGEIST, A WITCH, POP TOP PUMPKIN PEOPLE AND A BOTTLE CAP
CREATURE POSITION THEMSELVES ON STAGE. TOGETHER THEY RECITE A
POEM.

OCTOBER GROUP:

TWO BRIGHT ORANGE CAPS
AND SOME THICK TACKY GLUE,
A FEW FEET OF YARN AND
SOME FABRIC PAINT TOO!
A GREEN PUSH-PULL TOP,
AND A PATTERN TO TRACE,
A WIDE TOOTHY GRIN
ON A HOT ORANGE FACE.
PLUCKED FROM THE TRASH
INSTEAD OF A PATCH,
MAKE ONE FOR YOURSELF,
OR MAKE A WHOLE BATCH!

FROM UNDER THE TRASH
THAT'S PILED OUTSIDE,
BOTTLE CAP SPIDERS,
JUST LOVE TO HIDE.
SELECT A DARK BLUE OR
PURPLE MILK CAP.
BEND CHENILLE STEMS AND
GLUE TO THE SCRAP.
THE PIECES ARE SET WITH
BALANCE AND SPACE.
WIGGLE EYES GLUED TO A
BLACK POM-POM FACE,
HE'S SNEAKY AND CREEPY
WITH LEGS YOU CAN BEND.
KEEP ONE FOR YOURSELF AND

GIVE ON TO A FRIEND!

TO TOP OFF THE FLASHLIGHTS
ON HALLOWEEN NIGHT,
THIS PLASTIC POLTERGEIST
GIVES YOU A FRIGHT!
WRAPPED IN THE WAX
FROM CEREAL BOXES,
HE WARDS OFF THE WITCHES
AND SPIRITS AND FOXES.
TRANSPARENT IN FORM
WITH A BOTTLE CAP HEAD,
HE'LL LIGHT UP THE WAY
ON THE NIGHT THAT YOU DREAD.

STAGE DIRECTION:
AT THIS POINT, THE CHILDREN STOMP THEIR FEET
TO THE BEAT OF THIS LAST STANZA.

(FEET STOMPS AT UNDERLINEDWORDS)

OCTOBER GROUP:

HALLOWEEN IS THE <u>SCENE</u>
FOR BOTTLE CAP <u>BATS,</u>
2-LITER <u>TERRORS</u> AND
BOTTLE CAP <u>CATS,</u>
THEY'RE <u>SCARY</u> AND HAIRY
RECYCLED FROM <u>LIDS,</u>
TO FRIGHTEN <u>ADULTS</u> AND
CREATED BY <u>KIDS!</u>

STAGE DIRECTION:
All students shout in unison:
All:
GO REBIRTH! SAVE THE EARTH!
SIMPLIFY YOUR PLAN.
GO REBIRTH! SAVE THE EARTH!
EVERYBODY CAN!

NOVEMBER

STAGE DIRECTION:

AS THE OCTOBER GROUP LEAVES THE STAGE, THE BALLERINAS CARRY A BOTTLE CAP CORNACOPIA POSTER ACROSS THE STAGE. CHILDREN DRESSED IN INDIAN AND PILGRIM COSTUMES POSITION THEMSELVES ON STAGE TO SING, "A SACRED LOAN".

A SACRED PRAYER LYRICS AND SHEET MUSIC

NOVEMBER GROUP:

WE BOWS OUR HEADS
IN GRATEFUL PRAYER.
FOR BLESSINGS THAT
WE HAVE TO SHARE.
REMEMBERING PAST TIMES BEFORE,
WHEN HAVING LESS
MEANT WORKING MORE.

TIMES WERE HARD
BUT PEOPLE KNEW,
CONSERVATION
SAW THEM THROUGH.
THINGS WERE USED
TIME AND TIME AGAIN.
THERE WAS SO LITTLE
THEY COULD SPEND.

CHORUS:
THE INDIANS GAVE FRIENDSHIP
AND KNOWLEDGE OF THE LAND.
PILGRIMS GAVE THEM PRESENTS
AND IDEAS THEY HAD PLANNED.
UNITED IN THEIR JOURNEY,
THEY FOUND A BETTER WAY,
WE FOLLOW THEIR EXAMPLE,
ON THIS THANKSGIVING DAY.

THIS PLANET THAT WE CALL OUR OWN,
IS JUST A GIFT A SACRED LOAN.
THAT WE RETURN WHEN WE ARE DONE,
IT BELONGS TO EVERYONE!
WE MUST TREAT IT WITH RESPECT,
NUTURE IT WITHOUT NEGLECT.
PASS IT DOWN THE WAY IT CAME.
SO THE WORLD REMAINS THE SAME!

CHORUS:
THE INDIANS GAVE FRIENDSHIP
AND KNOWLEDGE OF THE LAND.
PILGRIMS GAVE THEM PRESENTS
AND IDEAS THEY HAD PLANNED.
UNITED IN THEIR JOURNEY,
THEY FOUND A BETTER WAY,
WE FOLLOW THEIR EXAMPLE,
ON THIS THANKSGIVING DAY.

STAGE DIRECTION:
All students shout in unison:

All:
GO REBIRTH! SAVE THE EARTH!
SIMPLIFY YOUR PLAN.
GO REBIRTH! SAVE THE EARTH!
EVERYBODY CAN!

"SACRED PRAYER" - 6th Song, November

DECEMBER

STAGE DIRECTION:

AS THE NOVEMBER GROUP LEAVE THE STAGE, THE BALLERINAS CARRY A
BOTTLE CAP CHRISTMAS TREE ACROSS THE STAGE. AS THEY CROSS, A
DRUMMER BOY, SIX ANGELS AND SANTA WITH A BOTTLE CAP BEARD
TAKE CENTER STAGE. THIS GROUP SINGS,
"CHRISTMAS IS THERE ALL AROUND YOU".

**CHRISTMAS IS THERE ALL AROUND YOU
LYRICS AND SHEET MUSIC**

DECEMBER GROUP:

THE RIBBONS AND WRAPPINGS, AND ALL OF THE TRAPPINGS,
THE HOLIDAYS BRING, CAN ASTOUND YOU!
LOOK THROUGH DIFFERENT EYES, AND TO YOUR SURPRISE,
CHRISTMAS IS THERE ALL AROUND YOU!
PLASTIC ANGEL DOLLS, DECORATE ALL THE HALLS,
FABRIC SOFTNER BELLS ON THE TABLE.
A WREATH MADE FROM CAPS, PAINTED PERHAPS,
A LAUNDRY SCOOP CUP FOR A STABLE.

CHORUS:
CHRISTMAS IS THERE ALL AROUND YOU,
IT JUST DOESN'T COME FROM A STORE.
HAPPINESS SPRINGS BY RECYCLING THINGS,
GIVING THEM MEANS SO MUCH MORE.
SO LOOK AROUND IN THE CORNERS,
FIND TREASURES WHEREVER YOU CAN.
USING THINGS TWICE, CAN BE VERY NICE,
JUST MAKE IT A PART OF YOUR PLAN!

JINGLE BELL LIDS, IMPRESS ALL THE KIDS,
SANTAS WITH BOTTLE CAP HEADS.
DISHWASHER BOYS, AND BOTTLE CAP TOYS,
SCOOPS ARE CONVERTED TO SLEDS!
ORNAMENT TOPS, CREATED FROM POPS
SNOWMEN FROM 2-LITER PLASTIC
WITH HOLIDAY THEMES, AND BOTTLE CAP DREAMS,
WE'VE STARTED SOMETHING FANTASTIC!

CHORUS:
CHRISTMAS IS THERE ALL AROUND YOU,
IT JUST DOESN'T COME FROM A STORE.
HAPPINESS SPRINGS BY RECYCLING THINGS,
GIVING THEM MEANS SO MUCH MORE.

SO LOOK AROUND IN THE CORNERS,
FIND TREASURES WHEREVER YOU CAN.
USING THINGS TWICE, CAN BE VERY NICE,
JUST MAKE IT A PART OF YOUR PLAN!

YOU CAN CHANGE WHAT YOU SEE! RECYCLE LIKE ME!
THE BOTTLE CAPS SHOW YOU THE WAY.
JUST EMPOWER THE KIDS! POP THE TOPS! SAVE THE LIDS!
FOR TOMORROW, BEGINS, HERE TODAY!

STAGE DIRECTION:
All students shout in unison:

All:
GO REBIRTH! SAVE THE EARTH!
SIMPLIFY YOUR PLAN.
GO REBIRTH! SAVE THE EARTH!
EVERYBODY CAN!

STAGE DIRECTION:
AT THIS POINT, THE DECEMBER GROUP LEAVE THE STAGE. DURING THE LAST SONG, "TOMORROW'S CHILDREN" TWO CHILDREN AT A TIME WILL CARRY THE POSTERS BACK ON STAGE DURING EACH STANZA FORMING A LINE OF POSTERS ACROSS THE FRONT OF THE STAGE.
JANUARY AND FEBRUARY COME OUT DURING THE 1ST STANZA,
MARCH AND APRIL DURING THE 1ST CHORUS,
MAY AND JUNE DURING THE 2ND STANZA,
JULY AND AUGUST DURING THE 2ND CHORUS,
SEPTEMBER AND OCTOBER DURING THE 3RD STANZA
AND NOVEMBER AND DECMBER DURING THE 3RD CHORUS.

TOMORROWS CHILDREN LYRICS AND SHEET MUSIC

WHOLE CAST:

TOMORROW'S CHILDREN WILL LIVE AND PLAY, (AND PLAY)
WITHIN THE WORLD, (THE WORLD)
WE MOLD TODAY. WHAT WE DO, AND HOW WE LIVE,
 (WE LIVE)

(((((JAN. AND FEB POSTERS.))))))))))))))

WILL DETERMINE WHAT WE GIVE.
BY CHANGING HOW WE THINK AND LEARN, (AND LEARN)
WE'LL GIVE MUCH MORE,
IN OUR RETURN. (RETURN)
GIVE THEM A CHANCE,
TO LIVE AS WE DO, (WE DO)
IT'S IN YOUR HANDS, IT'S ALL UP TO YOU!

WHOLE CAST:
TOMORROW'S CHILDREN HAVE TO KNOW,
THAT WE DIDN'T JUST LET GO,

(((((((MARCH AND APRIL POSTERS.))))))

LET THEIR FUTURE SLIP AWAY.
THEY NEED US RIGHT HERE TODAY.
WE MUST TAKE THIS URGENT CALL,
STAND UP STRAIGHT BEFORE WE FALL.
WE CAN DO IT IF WE TRY,
UNITED WE CAN ALL GET BY.

WHOLE CAST:
TOMORROW CHILDREN DESERVE A PLACE, (A PLACE)
CLEAN AND FREE (AND FREE) WITH LOTS OF SPACE.

((((((((((MAY AND JUNE POSTERS.))))))))))))

ROOM TO GROW AND PLAY AND RUN,
(AND RUN)
JUST LIKE US, WHEN WE HAVE FUN.
WE MUST KEEP THEM IN OUR PLAN, (OUR PLAN)
WHEN WE RECYCLE EVERY CAN,
BOTTLES JARS AND PLASTIC LIDS,
 (AND LIDS)
DO IT FOR THE FUTURE KIDS!

WHOLE CAST:
TOMORROW'S CHILDREN HAVE TO KNOW,
THAT WE DIDN'T JUST LET GO,

(((((((((**JULY AND AUGUST POSTERS.**))))))))))))

LET THEIR FUTURE SLIP AWAY.
THEY NEED US RIGHT HERE TODAY.
WE MUST TAKE THIS URGENT CALL,
STAND UP STRAIGHT BEFORE WE FALL.
WE CAN DO IT IF WE TRY,
UNITED WE CAN ALL GET BY.

WHOLE CAST:

EXCHANGE IDEAS, SHARE AND GROW, (AND GROW)
THE MORE YOU LEARN, (YOU LEARN)
THE MORE YOU KNOW.

(((((((((**SEPT. AND OCT. POSTERS**)))))))))))

EVERYDAY JUST DO YOUR PART, (YOUR PART)
AT HOME IS A GOOD PLACE TO START.
EDUCATE YOUR MOM AND DAD, (AND DAD)
SHOW THEM ALL THE FUN YOU HAD,
WHEN YOU RECYCLE JUST FOR FUN, (FOR FUN)
A LITTLE BIT HELPS EVERYONE!

WHOLE CAST:
TOMORROW'S CHILDREN HAVE TO KNOW,
THAT WE DIDN'T JUST LET GO

((((((((((**NOV. AND DEC. POSTERS.**))))))))))))

LET THEIR FUTURE SLIP AWAY.
THEY NEED US RIGHT HERE TODAY.
WE MUST TAKE THIS URGENT CALL,
STAND UP STRAIGHT BEFORE WE FALL.
WE CAN DO IT IF WE TRY,
UNITED WE CAN ALL GET BY.

"TOMORROW'S CHILDREN" - 8th Song, Finale

202

All students shout in unison:
All:
GO REBIRTH! SAVE THE EARTH!
SIMPLIFY YOUR PLAN.
GO REBIRTH! SAVE THE EARTH!
EVERYBODY CAN!

STAGE DIRECTION:
AT THIS POINT ALL OF THE POSTERS ARE LINED UP ACROSS THE STAGE IN
ORDER. THE POSTER PEOPLE KNEEL DOWN WHILE HOLDING THE POSTERS.
BETTY AND BILLY JOE BOTTLE CAP STEP FORWARD FROM OPPOSITE SIDES OF
THE STAGE TO END THE PROGRAM.

Finale

BOTTLECAPS: NOW EVERYBODY KNOWS ABOUT RECYCLING!

CLASS: (LET'S HEAR IT!)

BOTTLECAPS: TURNING ALL THE GARBAGE INTO CASH.

CLASS: (YOU KNOW IT!)

BOTTLECAPS: SAVING ALL THE ARTICLES THEY ASK FOR.

CLASS: (WITH SPIRIT)

BOTTLECAPS: CONDENSING ALL THE ITEMS IN THE TRASH.

CLASS: (DON'T THROW IT!)

BOTTLECAPS: NOW EVERYBODY KNOWS ABOUT THE PLASTIC

CLASS: (THE BOTTLES?)

BOTTLECAPS: NO, NOT THE BOTTLES BUT THE LIDS.

CLASS: (THAT'S RIGHT NOW!)

BOTTLECAPS: THEY'RE FILLING UP THE LANDFILLS ON THE PLANET.

CLASS: (WE KNOW IT!)

BOTTLECAPS: IT'S TIME TO EMPOWER ALL THE KIDS.

CLASS: (WITH ACTION!)

BOTTLECAPS: WE'VE FORMED A BOTTLE CAP COALITION!

CLASS: (WE'RE READY!)

BOTTLECAPS: SAVING ALL THE PLASTIC CAPS WE FIND!

CLASS: (YOU GOT IT!)

BOTTLECAPS: IN EVERY HOME IN THE CITY.

CLASS: (LET'S DO IT!)

BOTTLECAPS: WE'LL START BY RECYCLING THE MIND!

CLASS: (YOU KNOW IT!)

BOTTLECAPS: WE'VE MADE PROJECTS FROM THE BOTTLE CAPS
                    COLLECTED!

CLASS: (THE COLORS!)

BOTTLECAPS: EACH MONTH WE HAVE MADE A BRAND NEW THEME.

CLASS: (FOR SEASONS!)

BOTTLECAPS: AND WE TAUGHT WHAT WE LEARNED TO OUR PARENTS

CLASS: (WE SHOWED EM!)

BOTTLECAPS: INTRODUCED THEM TO THE BOTTLE CAPPING DREAM!

CLASS: (WE DID IT!)

TEACHERS:

Please copy and use the following certificate to reward the students
after their performance. Save the bottle caps you used to design new costumes
and projects for Earth Day next year!

GO REBIRTH! SAVE THE EARTH!

Building a Bridge of Hope

It is more important than ever for everyone to look into ways in which we can preserve our precious planet. In my own small way, I hope to contribute ideas to help utilize plastic bottle caps in various ways that promote education and recycling. My son, who is in seventh grade this year had to develop a project for Science class using everyday materials.

What a great opportunity for a bottle cap bridge to be born! This craft not only helped him understand design and math but it was fun too and makes for a wonderful gift as the bridge itself can be used as a small shelf!
Let's make a promise to each other and the planet to build a bridge to a better tomorrow!

TO MAKE THIS CRAFT YOU NEED:

4   DISHWASHING LIQUID PUSH-PULL TOPS
20 PLASTIC 2-LITER BOTTLE CAPS (SAME SIZE)
1 SHEET OF LIGHT BROWN FELT
LOW MELT GLUE GUN
64 POPSICLE STICKS
ANTIQUING WASH (TERRA COTTA)

TO BEGIN:
1.   Wash and dry all bottle caps. Cut the felt into 20 strips, the width and length of each cap.

glue felt to the outer diameter of each cap

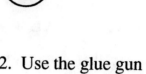

2. Use the glue gun to secure the strip around the diameter of each cap and cut away any excess.

3. Begin gluing the 10 bottle caps in an arc by the outer diameters so that the caps are held together by the felt. Repeat this procedure with the remaining caps to form another arc.

4. To stabalize the foundation of the bridge, pop the peaks off of the dishwashing liquid tops and use the bottom portion only and glue each one at the first cap of each arc.

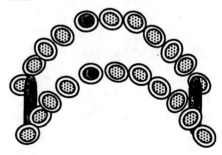

5. Use the length of a popsicle stick to connect the two arcs. One on each side by gluing the popsicle sticks directly to the felt.

6. To form the base of the bridge, glue 8 popsicle sticks side by side to the connecting stick. Repeat this procedure and overlap them in the middle and secure in place with glue.

7. Connect the two arcs by gluing a popsicle stick across the bridge in between each cap. You should have 9 connecting sticks.

8. To form the covering across the top of your beautiful bridge, glue popsicle sticks side by side on top of the caps all the way across the top.

GO
REBIRTH!
SAVE
THE
EARTH!

Printed in the United States
1013500001B